THE POCKET GUIDE TO TABLE TENNIS TACTICS

David Fairholm

The Pocket Guide to Table Tennis Tactics
was designed and edited by
Holland & Clark Limited, London

Designer
Julian Holland

Editor
Philip Clark

Artist
Martin Smillie

Photo Credit
Ian Ball

Cover photo by Ian Ball: (foreground) Istvan Jonyer (Hungary), against Ulf Thorsell (Sweden)

Published by Bell & Hyman
Denmark House, 37/39 Queen Elizabeth Street,
London SE1 2QB

First published in 1985

British Library Cataloguing in Publication Data
Fairholm, David
The pocket guide to table tennis tactics.
1. Table tennis
I. Title
796.34'6 GV1005

ISBN 0-7135-2538-X

Phototypeset in Great Britain by
Tradespools Limited, Frome, Somerset

Produced in Great Britain by
The Bath Press, Avon

Acknowledgements
Of the many individuals and organizations that helped with the preparation of this book, the author and publishers would particularly like to thank the English Table Tennis Association, Digital Ltd, Colin Wilson, and the Dunlop Sports Co Ltd for permission to reproduce the Dunlop Skills Award Scheme.

Contents

Introduction

Almost everybody has played table tennis at one time or another, whether at home, at the local social club or sports centre, or at a registered table tennis club.

Very often at the local sports centre you can see a couple of table tennis tables in use, where players, dressed in jeans and T-shirts, are patting the ball to and fro and having an enjoyable time.

It is sometimes argued that table tennis is a cheap, low-skill sport which requires little physical exertion, mental agility or tactical awareness. As a result, table tennis suffers from a poor public image. But it is not always played in such circumstances. When two top-class table tennis players get together they may be required to strike two balls in any one second. In fact, the world speed record for one minute is 163 hits between two players – incredibly almost three balls per second. This record is held by G. Sandley and D. Douglas (England) and was set at Eastbourne in 1984.

In fact, at its highest levels, table tennis is a thrilling, high speed, exceptionally skilful sport which is enjoyed by many millions of players worldwide.

When you consider that a table tennis ball can be struck at speeds of over 90 mph (145 kph) and returned safely, and can be spun at around 30 revolutions per second, you will understand that table tennis is one of the great speed and spin sports.

This book aims to help all keen players to achieve their full potential. The book emphasises the need for a sound technical base, and there are sections on physical fitness, training, match preparation and the role of the coach.

Once you have developed a sound foundation you can start to work on your tactical game. All the main areas of tactics are covered in a series of sections on such areas as assessing your opponent and learning how to outwit different types of player; analysing your own strengths and weaknesses and improving specific features especially tactics for service and return of service.

If you study the sections carefully and adapt them to your own needs you will develop your skills as a tactician and, I hope, will become master of your game.

Good luck!

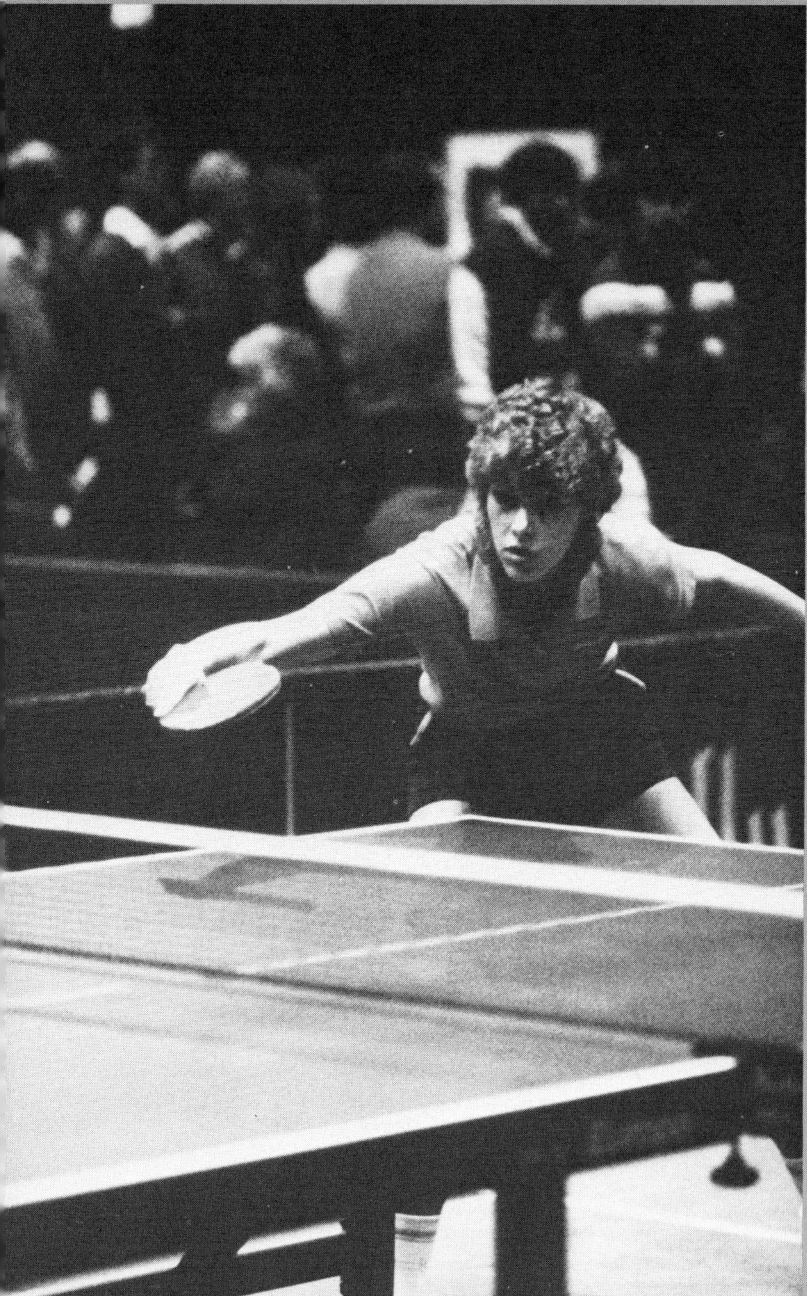

The International Scene

Table tennis is a major international sport. In 1983, the World Championship, held in Japan, was the second largest gathering of countries outside the Olympic Games.

Table tennis today is totally dominated by the Chinese – not surprisingly, since it is their national sport and they can boast more players than the rest of the world put together.

After a decade in the wilderness the Russians are back in the forefront led by twice European Champion Valentina Popova and the brilliant young Andrei Mazunov.

Nigeria would probably take the vote for the most improved nation, while the Canadians have made tremendous strides thanks to their importation of foreign stars.

The United States

However, one country that might have been expected to have capitalized on the sport but has not done so is the USA. Table tennis is an all-weather game, and with the harsh winters suffered in North America, it would seem highly suitable, especially since the two major indoor winter sports – ice hockey and basketball – are both team games.

Yet despite the Americans' lack of attention to the sport nationally they still have two players in the world top 100 in Danny Seemiller and Eric Boggan.

Not that table tennis is totally neglected in the USA. American Open Championships attract the very best players from China, Sweden and Japan, to name but three of the top countries.

If the sporting bodies in the United States put the same kind of energy into table tennis as they have already done with tennis and swimming, it is not hard to imagine their success.

The British Problem

Table tennis is still a minority sport in Britain. This seems to be partly because by tradition Britain concentrates its sporting resources on team games such as football, rugby, hockey and cricket, while individual sports seem not to have been so well catered for.

With limited equipment, teachers and finance, it makes sense to have many children on a sports field together under one games teacher. This may also help to explain the relative lack of British Olympic medals in general compared with the Eastern Bloc countries and the USA, where emphasis is often on individual sports.

Opportunities for the Future

As a result, table tennis, like many individual sports, is often ignored without being seriously considered. This is very unfortunate, as it is an extremely versatile sport.

For example, a school gym will easily accommodate six table tennis tables. Thus, with four players per table, 24 players can simultaneously learn this individual sport, no matter what the weather and all under the direction of one games teacher.

Sport in Britain could get far more out of table tennis, and it is time sports educationalists gave more people the opportunity to learn to play it. In Sweden, for example, with a population of only eight million, there are more players registered than in the UK, and the Swedes have produced several World and European champions in recent years.

A 'High-fidelity' Sport

It is interesting to record that table tennis is a high-fidelity sport, which means that once someone has become interested, they are likely to remain involved for many more years than in most other sports. This is a tribute to the sport itself, and demonstrates that, very often, table tennis is for life.

Technique and Tactics

Before we delve into the world of table tennis tactics, a word of advice. Beware the use of tactics which inhibit the quality of your strokes or the balance of your game. This may be necessary in the middle of an important match, but to make a habit of this may limit your overall technique.

Possible disadvantages are twofold.

First, you may be unable to carry out your desired tactics because of the limitations of your technique. Secondly, your opponent's range of tactics is widened by your technical weakness.

By all means use tactics wisely to give you victories which would otherwise be defeats, but try to ensure that your tactics are based on solid technical foundations.

Tactics and technique are interrelated and, in order to make use of tactics, it is necessary to have already developed confidence, control and consistency of stroke production. After all, in a competition there is no time to work on, or worry about technique.

Always remember that technique comes first and tactics later. For whatever range of strokes you use, you will require the utmost confidence; and for whatever range of strokes you play against, you will require the utmost understanding.

Key:

f/h	forehand
b/h	backhand
f/d	forehand drive
b/d	backhand drive
f/l	forehand loop
b/l	backhand loop
L	left
R	right
X	crossover point

The Main Strokes

Constant Display

Before discussing strokes, the weapons that you are likely to use or have to play against, you need to understand and develop 'constant display'. This is a basic technical principle of efficient body movement in table tennis. It means that the eyes remain at a constant vertical height during each rally. The body's centre of gravity is therefore stable, giving good balance, and your view of the table and opponent is clear.

Constant display. The head and eyes remain at a constant height enhancing good movement and even display.

Good use of this principle means that, as you prepare to play your stroke, all your physical adjustments are tactical (deceptive), not technical (giving cues to your opponent).

The Strokes

Your weapons in table tennis are the main strokes that you are likely to play or play against. There are five 'mother strokes'. These are:

1. Backhand Push

This is a safety or sparring stroke, used for control while searching for an advantage. It is reliable and useful in service return, but is not usually a point winner, giving the opponent time to play.

Backhand push 1. The backswing for the backhand push, the basis for all play on the backhand side. The non-playing arm aids balance throughout the action.

Backhand push 2. Careful contact on the backhand push.

Backhand push 3. The follow-through is short.

2. Forehand Push

As above, but more difficult to master. In top-class table tennis many services are played short to the forehand to encourage a forehand push return.

Forehand push 1. Possibly the most difficult of the four basic strokes as distance and body awareness are crucial. But, like its counterpart, the backhand push, it is a very useful sparring stroke. This shows the preparation of this very short stroke.

Forehand push 2. Note good space between elbow and body.

Forehand push 3. The follow-through moving into a ready position.

3. Backhand Drive

This is the quickest stroke in table tennis, a fast, attacking stroke. It is difficult to anticipate its placement because of the use of wrist, but lacks power.

Backhand drive 1. Shown here the backswing for possibly the fastest stroke – the backhand drive. The elbow is at 90 degrees, as in all four basic strokes. This gives maximum control.

Backhand drive 2. On contact. The wrist turns for accurate placement.

Backhand drive 3. A good follow-through with left shoulder forward.

4. Forehand Drive

The most powerful stroke. It is a major weapon, since it is most often the point-winner. It is a long stroke, however, requiring time to recover, and is difficult to play when the ball is very close to the body.

Forehand drive 1. The backswing for the forehand drive – the most powerful weapon in a player's armoury. The legs are bent and the body leans forwards. The player leans into the ball for extra power.

Forehand drive 2. Just after contact – retaining a constant display.

Forehand drive 3. The follow-through. The bat follows the ball's arc.

5. Service

Service is the first opportunity of winning the point. It is the only time a player has total control of the rally, therefore making it a closed skill (one in which anticipation is not involved). At a high level 70% of the points are won by the server, since the stroke can win the point outright or else dictate the tactics for the remainder of the rally.

If you do not use your service to the best advantage, you can be sure that your opponent will.

Backhand service.

Good preparation for a backhand serve which will incorporate backspin and side spin. The player stoops to give himself plenty of room to operate. It's vital for the wrist to remain unrestricted for a smooth action.

The contact. Look for maximum speed on touch.

Total freedom in this good follow-through.

Forehand service.

Getting down for a forehand side spin serve.

A perfect throw-up makes contact so much easier.

Forehand side spin service.

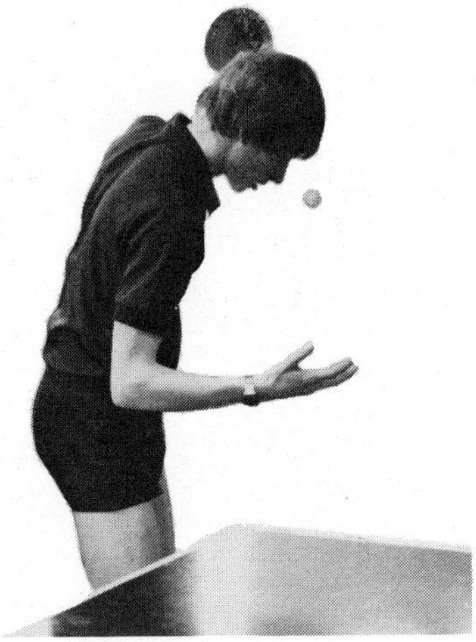

The most common serve – the forehand side spin serve.

Good disguise – did it contain topspin or backspin?

Further strokes

All strokes in table tennis develop from the five mother strokes. The most common ones are:

1. Forehand Topspin (loop)

The most widely used attacking stroke. There are many variations and it is a difficult stroke for the opponent to control. Its weaknesses are that it is easy to mistime and cannot be played from a short ball.

The forehand loop. Nearly everyone's favourite stroke. This is the follow-through to the intermediate loop (see page 63).

2. Backhand Topspin (loop)

Not so common as the forehand loop or backhand drive. It can be well disguised and very spinny, but it lacks power and is very difficult to time correctly.

The backhand loop just prior to contact. Note the wrist is limp and ready to 'snap' on contact.

3. Forehand Smash
The most powerful weapon. It normally wins the point directly but may be blocked past you if your opponent reacts quickly enough.

Plenty of backswing, plenty of body, plenty of acceleration for this smash which should end the rally.

4. Backhand Smash
This avoids the need to cover the whole table with the forehand when attacking, but is less powerful.

The upper body turns in anticipation to this backhand smash but the feet should remain square to the line of play for a quick recovery.

5. Forehand Flick and Backhand Flick
Used to attack a short ball. The flick opens up a rally from a tight service or push. It can be a point winner but if played slowly can allow the opponent to attack.

A text-book forehand flick. Notice the left leg goes under the table for maximum stability.

6. Forehand Chop and Backhand Chop

A defensive weapon played away from the table with backspin. It can cope with good attacking strokes, but is slow and not usually a point winner.

A much wider stance is required for all strokes away from the table – this will aid both control and consistency.

The ball is directly below the eyes, just before contact. Wide stance gives maximum control.

7. Forehand Block

This is useful when under pressure with little time to organize the body and thoughts. The block returns the ball quickly with little effort but can allow the opponent to follow up with another attacking stroke.

The forehand block. A useful stroke when you are caught out of position.

8. Backhand Block

This is easier and more useful than its forehand counterpart, since it is normally taken in front of the body on the half-volley. This gives the opponent little chance to recover. Good use of the wrist can turn the block into a well-disguised drive or topspin.

A quick backhand block just after contact. Very little body action is required which makes it an excellent reflex shot.

9. Forehand Drop Shot

Played when the opponent is away from the table. It is a point-winner if well disguised, but can be smashed if not kept low and short.

Forehand drop shot. An essential when dealing with defensive players. Elbow kept low for security and to keep the ball short.

Backhand drop shot. Like its counterpart you simply can't afford to miss. You must pay great attention to detail.

10. Backhand Drop Shot

Easier to control than the forehand, but it shows that you are not playing an attacking forehand.

Further strokes can be developed from those listed above. For example, sidespin can be added to all of them (especially service and loop) but the strokes mentioned cover the range of weapons available to you as a competitor.

Master of the Game

Most good players can play most of these strokes fairly well, but few can play all of them well. It is perhaps not good to try to master all these strokes, although an understanding of all of them is essential.

In competition, you and your opponent will have mastered some strokes and not others and this interaction is an important factor in determining tactics. If you play the strokes you have mastered and force your opponent to play ones that he hasn't, then you are the master of the game. Tactics are the means by which you achieve this.

Strategy and Tactics

What are tactics? What is strategy?

For our purposes tactics will refer to choices made in the competitive situation, while strategy will refer to a player's preparation or overall planning. We can then split strategy and tactics into four distinct areas.

These are:

1. Career strategy.
2. Seasonal strategy (periodisation).
3. Match preparation.
4. Match tactics.

Career Strategy

Many players (or their coaches) have some realization of their table tennis potential, and set themselves long-term aims from early in their career. Other players, however, choose to cross each bridge as it is reached. This is a personal choice which depends largely on ambition.

Seasonal Strategy

Most players have some plans or ambitions for each new table tennis season, especially with regard to particular events or opponents. On an international level, players need to perform at their peak in late autumn for the major international open events and in April for the World or European, Asian and American championships.

For all players there are particular times in the year when the aim is 'to provide the best opportunity to play at peak performance'.

Periodisation

This can be achieved by a programme of periodisation. Although it is a complex subject, the principle is very simple and without too much detail the graph (next page) gives an indication of the process.

Repeat for second cycle January to June.

Preparation

At the beginning of the preparation period, most of your training should be off the table with heavy emphasis on strength and condition, and a little technical work (consistency and regular footwork). Gradually your physical load should be lightened and based on speed rather than stamina, whilst technical work needs to increase and become more specific (irregular footwork, power, spin, service and return). In this way you can develop more subtle skills upon a solid technical base.

Competition

Later still, emphasis needs to be placed on tactical match play to produce your peak level of performance.

During the competitive phase when important matches are played, most work is tactical, simulating match situations. This is designed to maintain the peak.

When the competitive phase is over, you will need to rest, doing only physical work entirely outside table tennis. This is a regenerative phase which is necessary before you are ready for the next preparation period. This cycle can be used effectively once, or at most twice, in a season. No-one can guarantee that you will perform well on

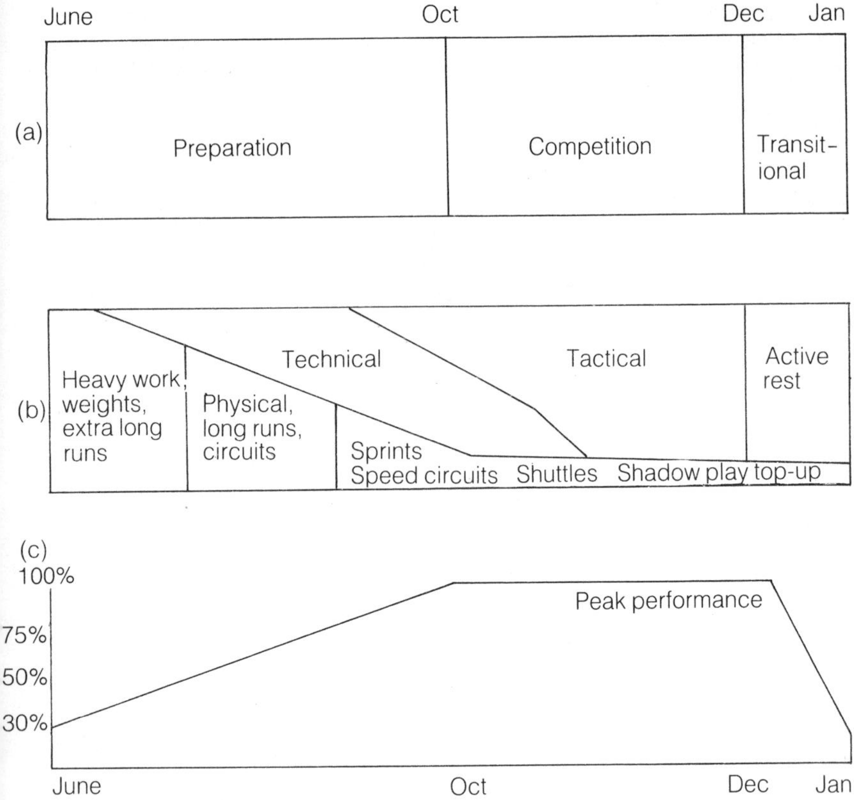

A typical periodisation programme. (a) The half year is divided into three areas. (b) Note the heavy physical work is completed by September and during the competition phase the technical work tapers off. (c) A player can't be at his peak the whole year.

a given day but periodisation is designed to give a player the best possible chance.

While working towards seasonal goals however, the immediate, lower priority events must not be overlooked. Careful preparation is necessary for all competition.

Match Preparation

Ideally, match preparation begins before match day. A player should be physically fit and technically sound. By match day it is too late!

It helps to acclimatize by duplicating match conditions. Try to find out what type of table you will be playing on, which brand of ball, the size of the room and the time of day. (Some world-class players are notoriously bad at playing in the mornings.) Perhaps you can arrange to practise under similar conditions but, if not, at least you will be aware of the situation beforehand.

Tactically, a player should have discovered who his likely opponents are and practised relevant set-pieces accordingly.

Warm-Ups

On the day of the match itself it is important to warm-up before going on court; a warm-up will increase flexibility and help reduce the risk of injury.

A muscle which has been extended and contracted on a number of occasions will also do so more forcefully than one working from cold.

Finally, neuro-muscular activity (shadow play) within the warm-up will groove the specific muscle patterns used in table tennis. All this will help to enhance your performance.

Static, Ballistic and Passive Stretching

Of the three types of warm-up, I would recommend a combination of static and semi-ballistic stretching.

Static stretching is reaching to your maximum and holding stationary for about 10 seconds, repeating twice to reach further.

Ballistic stretching is the old-fashioned jerking movement, pulling a muscle beyond its static limit.

Passive stretching is allowing your partner to stretch your muscles for you, while you relax.

Common sense is your best judge when balancing your warm-up. Personally, I dislike the ballistic type of warm-up, which if composed badly, gives more chance of injury than actually playing!

You and your coach, however, will know the best type of warm-up for you. Exercises need to be tailored to your body, your personality and the prevailing situation. The exercises used for warm-up will vary according to the time of day (probably heavier in the morning), the temperature of the hall, the opportunity to practise on the table and even the type of opponent.

Having warmed-up, try to knock-up as much as possible before your match, in order to acclimatize to the speed and bounce of the ball in the prevailing conditions.

Physical Fitness

Physical fitness is vital for sustaining periods of good quality play and as such it warrants a high priority. The obvious analogy to a player who prepares physically is the car which is regularly serviced. It performs well with less chance of a breakdown.

Mental preparation

While you are preparing physically, do not ignore your mental approach. It is the same as physical preparation in as much as it has to be practised. It would be easy to write a whole book on mental practice! However, there are two major advantages to being well prepared mentally.

Firstly, if you are technically, physically and generally well organized you will feel confident on the day. (Conversely, if you daydream in practice no doubt you will daydream in matches.)

Secondly, concentration is the awareness of *now* and it's important to be aware of *now* in practice, so you can be aware of *now*, in the important match, set, game, point, rally and stroke.

By simulating mental pressure in a practice situation it will prepare you for the big occasion.

My old coaching mentor Dave Lindley used to say, 'Hit every ball whether in a match or practice as if it was 20 all in the deciding game.'

Bad Conditions and Decisions

Table tennis is not played in a vacuum. The table, ball, lighting, floor, background, time etc. all have an influence on the match and a player needs to cope with many distractions. Common ones are:

1. The crowd are against you.
2. Balls fly across from other courts.
3. The opposing coach is shouting advice to his player.
4. The opponent keeps upsetting your rhythm by towelling down.
5. At the start of the second game you realize you now have worse light.
6. The umpire makes a bad decision for or against you.

There are positive and negative mental approaches to all these situations.

Bad Decisions

Try to leave *everything* to the umpire. In a confrontation don't say anything. Remember that there is one umpire and it is not you or the other player.

In this way you will sometimes win the argument and sometimes lose it, but you will never be branded a cheat, since you don't try to influence the umpire's decision.

Don't *admit* anything but don't *complain* either. If you admit that a ball touched the edge of the table, you are a *two-time loser* as your opponent will not always be so nice!

Like many other sports table tennis possesses its gamesmen and cheats. There's the player who cons the umpire by admitting to nets, edges and volleys when he is 19-6 up. By doing this, he hopes to get away with cheating in a tight game as the umpire has become confident of his honesty.

Your job is to keep playing and accept decisions. The umpire will probably make fewer mistakes than the players!

The approach to this situation which I'd recommend is to ignore everything as far as possible. If you become involved, you are not concentrating on the job in hand.

Generally speaking both players play under the same conditions. Even if they favour the other player it is very rarely that a player can honestly say that he was beaten by conditions and not his opponent.

When conditions are genuinely working for the opponent, the *total* player maximizes his probabilities

Desmond Douglas, England's top player for almost a decade, moves around the backhand court before getting in with a powerful forehand.

China's Guo Yao Hua was World Champion in 1981 and 1983 and is the greatest table tennis player I have ever seen.

of winning by adopting a good attitude.

The *total* player likes to prove to himself that he is unaffected by adverse conditions, gamesmanship etc, and gets more satisfaction from winning under conditions that suit the opponent rather than himself. It's like beating a *better* opponent.

Match Tactics

This is where tactics ultimately apply. Tactical thinking involves such questions as:

1. What type of bat does the opponent use?
2. What is his/her style?
3. Where are his/her strengths and weaknesses?
4. What have you learnt from watching him/her, and from the knock-up?
5. Should a player change a winning game? If so, when?
6. Can I identify his/her tactics?
7. Which end has the better light?
8. What do I do if I win the toss?

Answering these questions and any others you may ask yourself involves knowledge of *yourself*, your *opponent* and the *environment* in which you have to play.

You, Your Game and Your Coach

Once you have mastered the basics it is important to identify your personality on the table and your particular style of play. For example, English champion Desmond Douglas has a stable personality on the table, combined with speed and agility. As a result he can at world class level be loosely termed a 'blocker'.

Working with a coach can be very helpful. There are aspects of your game that you feel from within, which your coach cannot detect. Equally there are aspects that your coach can see which go unnoticed by you. Four eyes are better than two.

Analyse Your Game

With your coach, take stock of the present state of your game. List the strokes that you play and rank them. Be aware of your physical state, recognize its limitations and take stock of your mental attitude (remember that attack and defence are just states of mind).

In order to understand yourself and your game I offer below a simple system for monitoring performance in a match. Arm your coach with paper and pen and ask him to analyse the match in this way. After playing a few opponents some patterns will emerge.

With this information you should discover whether you win points on your service or against the service; in long rallies or short; at the beginning of a game or at the end; with your forehand loop or backhand push. This will help your judgement in a match.

Performance Monitoring Chart

Desmond Douglas (England) *v* Vladislav Broda (Czechoslovakia) English Open Final 1984

Point number	1st game (Douglas to serve)	2nd game (Broda)	3rd game (Douglas)	4th game (Broda)	5th game (Douglas)
1	3				
2	2				
3					
4					
50					

Each box represents every point in the match. The first point of the first game is recorded in the top left corner (Point No. 1, 1st game). Record the number of balls which hit the table.

For example, Douglas served first in this match. He served short, Broda returned and Douglas played a winning follow up which Broda could not return. Therefore, the number of 'good' balls was three (service, return, server's follow up). So the number 3 should be recorded in the appropriate square. For the second point, Douglas served and Broda returned a ball Douglas could not return. Therefore a 2 is recorded.

Desmond Douglas (England) *v* Vladislav Broda (Czechoslovakia)

Point number	1st game (Douglas to serve)	2nd game (Broda)	3rd game (Douglas)	4th game (Broda)	5th game (Douglas)
1	3	9	9	8	2
2	2	6	6	2	2
3	1	4	2	6	2
4	3	1	4	4	5
5	10 3–2	3 2–3	3 2–3	0 5–0	9 2–3
Change server every 5 points					
6	0	7	3	1	3
7	3	5	4	3	2
8	9	4	1	5	5
9	7	5	3	5	4
10	4 5–5	3 6–4	4 4–6	1 10–0	1 4–6
11	0	1	3	2	2
12	1	2	5	12	5
13	8	9	7	10	2
14	4	5	2	1	7
15	4 6–9	1 7–8	3 8–7	3 13–2	6 6–9
16	1	12	0	3	2
17	8	6	1	3	7
18	1	2	10	1	1
19	5	8	3	5	4
20	3 7–13	2 7–13	4 11–9	2 17–3	0 9–11
21	9	2	6	5	7
22	5	5	5	4	4
23	1	6	3	1	5
24	10	5	3	2	1
25	3 11–14	2 10–15	2 14–11	1 19–6	3 13–12
26	3	1	2	3	4
27	4	10	2	2	4
28	2	1	2	1	3
29	1	3	1	21–7	4
30	2 14–16	8 13–17	6 18–12	to Douglas	4 17–13
31	2	2	5		3
32	6	1	1		5
33	4	1	5		10
34	5	1	21–12		3
35	3 16–19	6 15–20	to Douglas		5
					21–14 to Douglas
36	1	3			
37	2	4			
38	1	16–21			
	17–21 to Broda	to Broda			

An odd number always means that the server has won the point and an even number that the receiver has won the point. Because the service changes every five points we know which player has won which point throughout the match. We can see that Broda served 83 times. He won 18 points *directly* from service (since there are 18 '1's when Broda was serving). He also won another 10 points with his follow up (there are 10 '3's attributed to him). Therefore, Broda won 34% of his points from his service and first attack.

Many other interesting patterns emerge after careful study of this chart. See what you can observe after just five minutes of analysis.

Long-term Potential

By now you should have discovered what type of game you play and in particular what you do under pressure. Some of the conclusions will probably surprise you! Before rushing off to the practice hall though, in order to iron out all known weaknesses, you will first need to assess the long-term potential of the components of your game.

Every part of a player's game has its own potential, and the combination of these parts gives the player's overall potential. Only the reckless player attempts to practise and perform beyond this unbreakable barrier. Training and coaching can improve a player's performance towards potential but neither can put in what nature left out!

Assessing Your Game

This assessment can be a tricky business since it requires a certain amount of crystal-ball gazing on the part of you and your coach. This is where mutual respect and trust are vital as you discuss the capabilities and limitations of your strokes, footwork, mental and physical condition, and so on.

Once you recognize the likely balance of your game and potential, you should begin to specialize in your development. If you will never chop in a match, never chop in practice. Equally if you ought to use a backhand loop but cannot perform it well, practise until it becomes an integral part of your game.

Strengths *v* Weaknesses

Occasionally you may under- or over-estimate your potential but you must be decisive.

There is a danger in spending too much of your time working on weaknesses, when these weaknesses are already nearing their potential. It is far better to concentrate more on developing strengths and working on openings for those strengths. In this way a player can hide weaknesses by dominating the play tactically and pre-empting attacks on his own weak points.

Theory into Practice

A structured training programme can be implemented within the periodisation model set out earlier (see page 22). It must always include table exercises and routines, physical training and selected competition (the details of training must ultimately be decided by player and coach).

Before discussing the role of the coach more fully however, there are two useful 'rules of thumb' which can be applied to all table tennis training.

Basic Rules for Practice Play

The first rule relates to the emphasis placed on each part of your game. You should always practise each stroke or combination of strokes in proportion to how frequently you expect to use them in competition (remember that you should allow for your long-term potential).

This will ensure for example, that there is heavy emphasis on service and return since this begins every rally.

The second rule relates to attitude to practice. Try to imagine match situations, even when practising simple consistency exercises. This will attune your mind to the pressure of competition and will cut down unforced errors. Unless you are a genius, form cannot be controlled like water from a tap. Most of us are creatures of habit and a critical but constructive attitude in practice will bring results in a match.

A lazy attitude in practice results only in unforced errors and such errors will be repeated and magnified when you are under pressure.

The Role of the Coach

Your coach can help you to develop towards your full potential as a player with trust, respect and constant attention. But the total coach has another equally important role, which is to ensure that the player can train and compete just as effectively in his absence.

Inevitably there will be occasions when the coach is not available, and it is the responsibility of the coach to cultivate self-sufficiency in the player. Moreover if a player is to make the grade at table tennis, he may represent his town, county, National League team or his country. During this progression he will play under the direction of the relevant team coach, not his personal, paternal coach.

Yet many players seem to perform well only in the company of the paternal coach. This is a serious weakness which speaks more for the attitude of the coach than that of the player.

If a player finds himself in this position it is for one of three reasons. Either his coach *is* the best in the whole world! Or the coach has discouraged alternative advice or the player has chosen to listen to only one person.

This extreme reliance on the coach is usually caused by the coach stifling the player and failing to prepare him for the harsh realities of what is essentially an *individual* sport.

The total player is able to per-

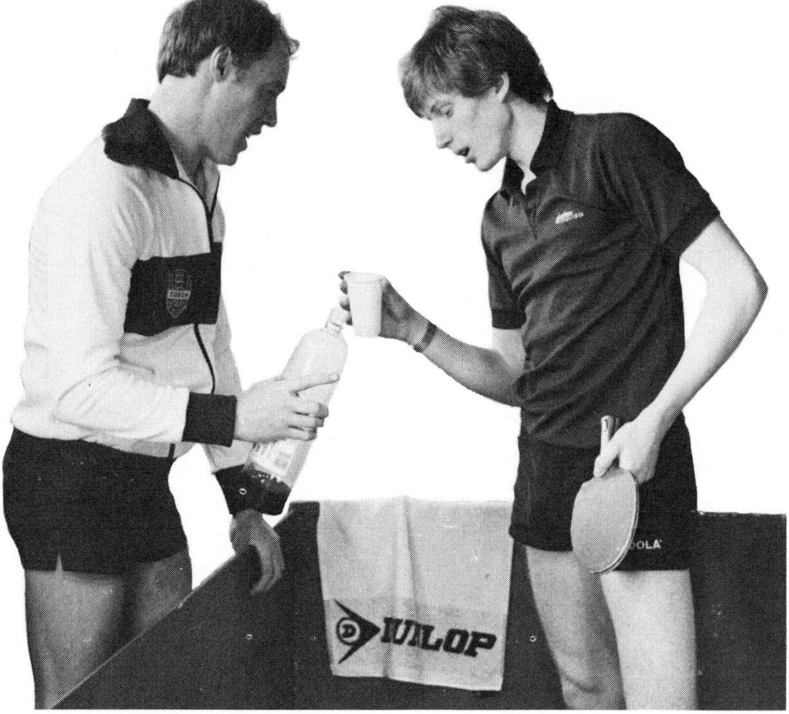

form well without a coach and is versatile enough to separate the wheat from the chaff when being advised by other coaches. The total coach is the one whose player achieves this versatility.

You only have one minute to give advice and encouragement, use it wisely. Information should include where a player is winning and losing points, whether a change of tactics is necessary and a forecast of the opponent's tactics.

Tactics Against All Opponents

In table tennis, there are tactics which can be used effectively against any opponent, no matter whether the opponent is world-class or a complete beginner. These general tactics exist for two reasons.

Firstly, all players are limited by the physical constants in table tennis, namely the dimensions of the table and the net. These are fixed (or invariable) from one match to the next.

This means for one example, that a ball which is struck from under net height can never be smashed. The laws of physics tell us that such a smash will travel into the net or off the end of the table. Even the world-class player must play this ball more slowly, so that gravity has time to pull the ball down on to the table.

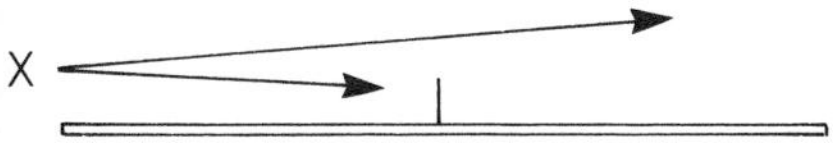

Impossible to smash

Secondly, all players to a greater or lesser extent are constrained by their physical limitations. For example, even the fastest man in the world needs *some* time to react, and can only cover ground at a certain speed.

This section includes many examples of such tactics and usually you will be able to use them to good advantage against anyone. It must be realized though, that general tactics are less effective against a higher standard of opponent. This is because the range of tactical options is narrowed by a better opponent and also because the execution of your tactics needs to be more exact.

If the tactics are based on good placement of the ball, an error of six inches (15 cm) may win the point against a weak opponent, whereas the stronger opponent may attack this ball. When playing a world-class opponent, the tactics must be executed perfectly to be of any use.

The real skill of tactics is timing. By sticking to your best tactic the whole time you would simply make it obvious to your opponent, who can then plan to overcome the tactic. Above all you are *predictable*. The secret is to use your obvious tactics in a less obvious way.

I like to think of a set of tactics as the series of boxes below.

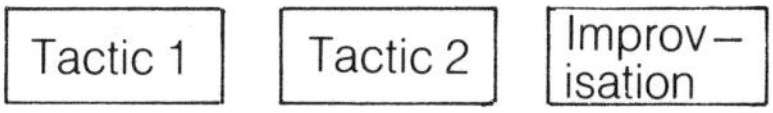

You may have a number of ideas, say placement, spin, speed, service and so on. Each of these ideas is contained in one box. Since you do not wish to be predictable the final box would be the box of improvisation.

Good tactics involves precise timing. In particular, knowing 'when to play in which box'. A good tactician knows when to stay in a box and when to move, so that the opponent is always left one mental step behind.

Switch Tactics

Intelligent switch play is usually a good tactic. The 'switch' is a change in the line of play, surprising the opponent. This can give a tremendous advantage allowing you to 'get in' with your most penetrating stroke (see Diagram 1).

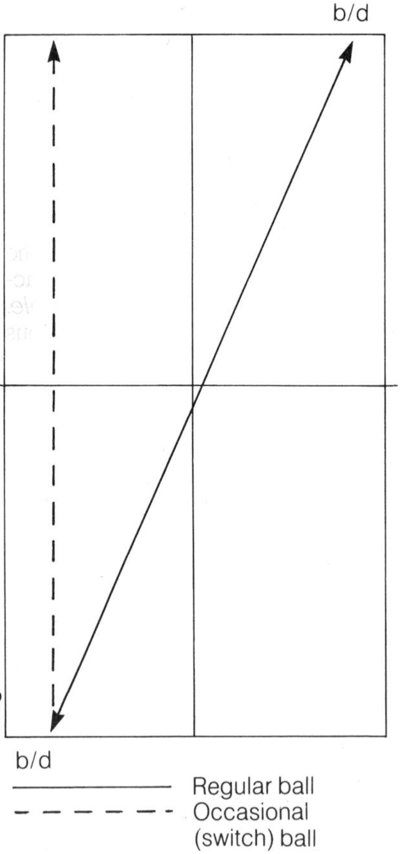

Diagram 1

Here two right-handed players are attacking each other with backhand drives across court. When the opponent least expects it, you play straight down the line. This normally results in a weak forehand which you then attack.

Switching the Switch

This is a deadly weapon if you stay close to the table. When your opponent switches he will probably move towards his backhand corner to get his forehand in. Your best tactic then is to switch-the-switch and play your forehand wide across court. This will normally catch the opponent out of position and halfway through his next stroke (Diagram 2).

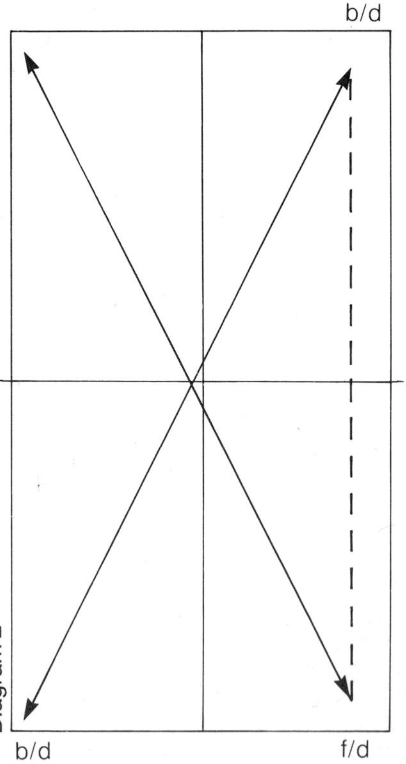

Diagram 2

Down the Line

Somewhere in the region of 80% of rally play is on the diagonal or a degree of diagonal (Diagram 3).

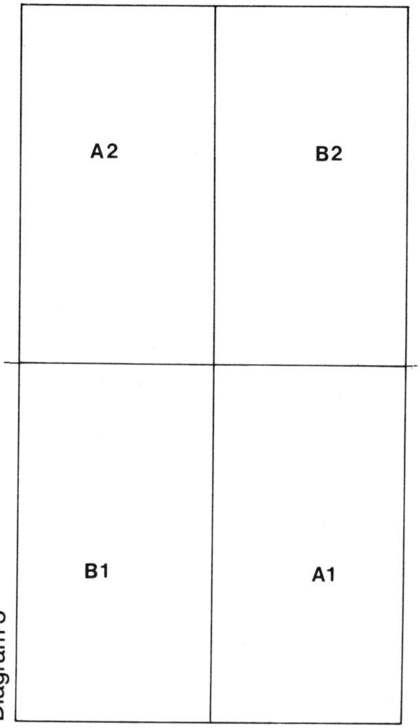

Diagram 3

This means that a ball which bounces in half **A1** will nearly always then be struck into half **A2.** Similarly **B1** is played into **B2**. Why do people naturally play this way? The answer is because it is easier! On the 9ft × 5ft (2.8m × 1.5m) table, Pythagoras tells us that the diagonal length is 10ft $3\frac{1}{2}$ in (3.16m) – more table to aim at. The natural body twist also lends itself to diagonal play.

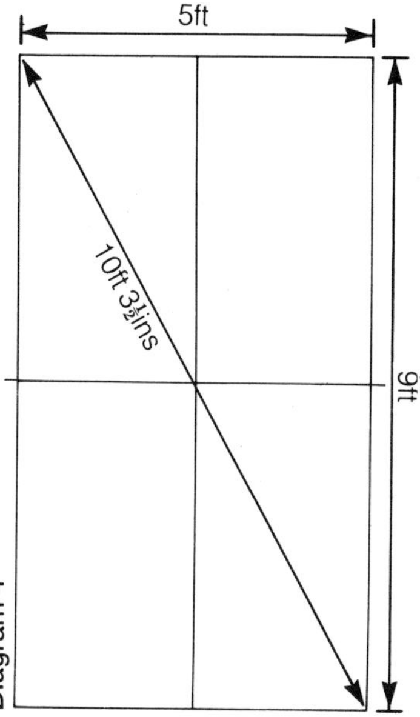

Diagram 4

The diagonal ball is the easier to play, but being longer gives the opponent more time. The ball down the line (from **A1** to **B2** or **B1** to **A2**) is more difficult to play but *even more difficult* to play against (see Diagrams 5 and 6).

Diagram 5

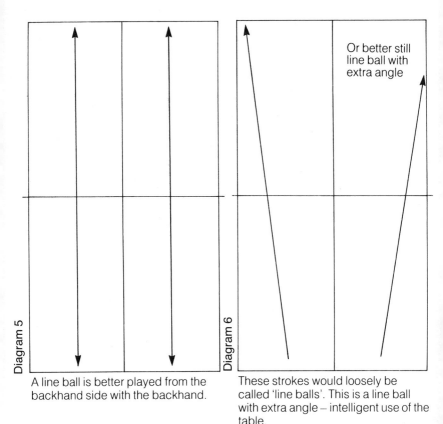

A line ball is better played from the backhand side with the backhand.

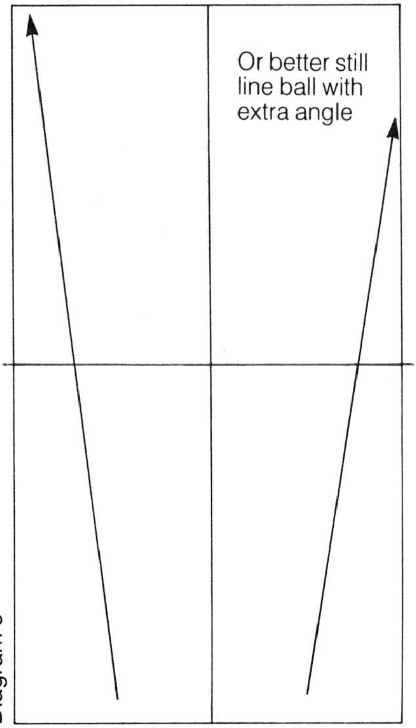

Diagram 6

These strokes would loosely be called 'line balls'. This is a line ball with extra angle – intelligent use of the table.

Playing down the line is one of the few times when backhand attacks will conquer the mighty forehand. The backhand is more pliable, less predictable and has easier recovery than the forehand.

In the right-hander's match, (see Diagram 7) where Player 1 and Player 2 are playing forehand loop to backhand drive down the line respectively, Player 2's switch is likely to be more effective than Player 1's. Try this as an exercise. The forehand player will feel extremely vulnerable on the backhand side.

It follows that your forehand attacks down the line must be strong enough to ensure a weak return or preferably no return at all. Conversely, feel confident of your backhand drive down the line – you are in total control enabling you to be master of the game (Diagram 8).

Diagram 7

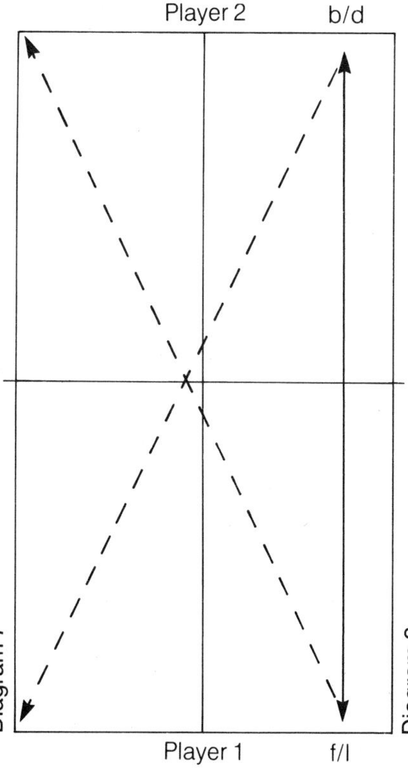

This practice demonstrates how the backhand can conquer the forehand. Broken lines = occasional switch.

Diagram 8

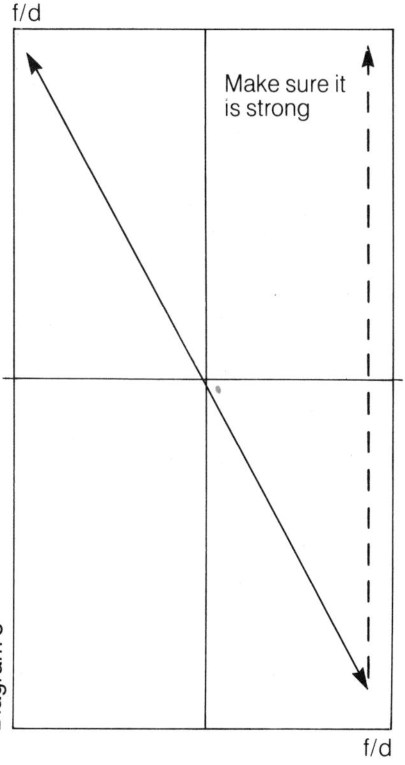

If you're going to switch from the diagonal with your forehand, it must be strong.

Tactics against Movement

It is often said that a player is poor on his feet but aren't we all sometimes? The usual advice is to move the ball around. This is not so simple, however, because weaknesses in movement vary from:

Moving to a wide ball.

Moving away from the ball.

Changing direction (stop-start acceleration).

Moving whilst already in motion.

Moving in to and away from the table.

Moving to a Wide Ball

This isn't really the problem that players seem to think because table tennis is a decision-making game. If a ball is played wide it is obvious

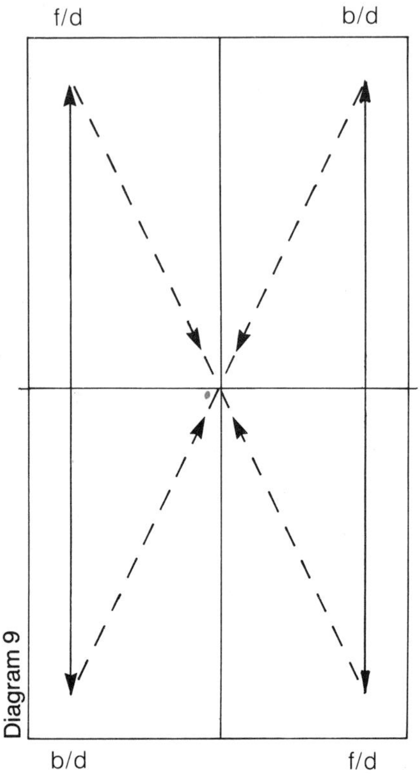

A useful switching practice

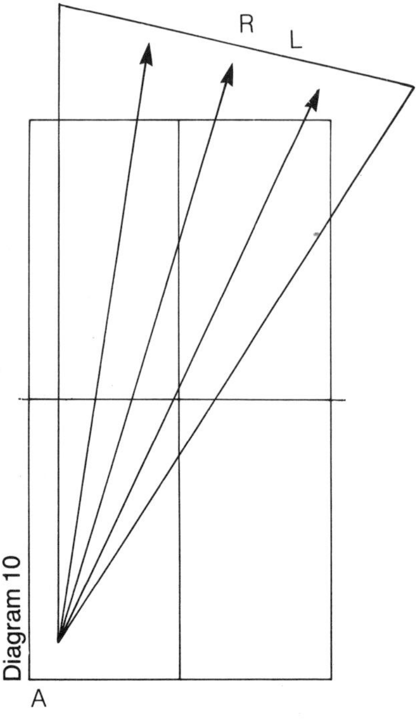

Maximum angle from A

that you have to go towards it. It is the subtler movements that tend to present problems as they cause indecision and require delicate movement.

It is nevertheless important to understand the angles of play which create the wide ball. Hopefully you will then have open spaces to aim at while the opponent is groping his way back into position.

Simply playing alternately to the backhand and forehand corners does not necessarily produce a wide ball at all.

Too much diagonal play restricts the angles of play. By playing diagonally in A and B (Diagrams 10, 11 and 12) you will fail to out-manoeuvre your opponent as he is able to cover all possibilities with little movement.

However, if you play a number of balls down the line and then go wide you will force your opponent out of position to play the line ball

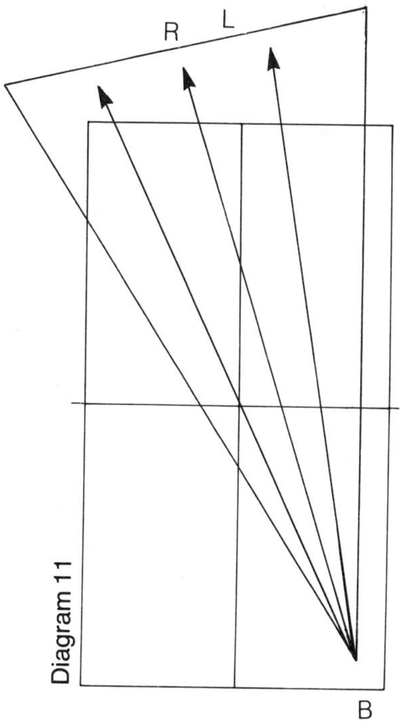

Maximum angle from B

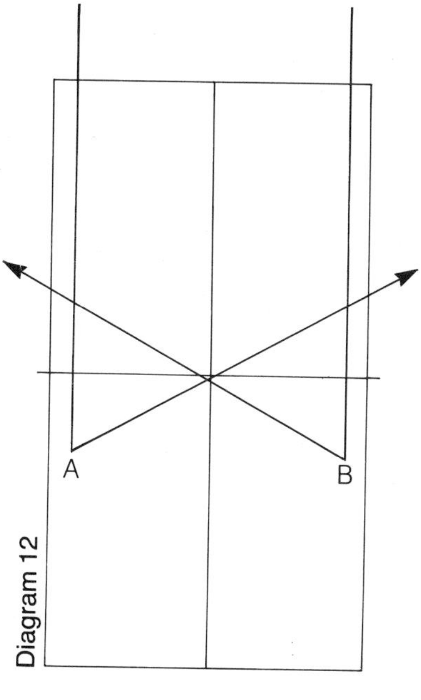

Maximum angle increases with a short ball

and then leave him with too much ground to cover (Diagrams 13 and 14).

In Diagram 15 the ball is played just off-centre to the forehand. The switch is then played wide to the forehand, creating a wider forehand angle.

In Diagram 16, the attacker is pinning the opponent on the backhand. As the opponent wants to move around his backhand to play his stronger forehand the wide switch is played just after he has committed himself to his 'run'. This is the best wide ball.

Moving Away from the Ball

A table tennis table is 5ft (1.54m) wide. The average player is perhaps 15" (38cm) wide, so it may appear that the wide ball is always a good shot to play. This is not so because a good low-crouched stance (like a goalkeeper receiving a penalty) will produce a 'turning circle' of around 5ft (1.54m) diameter (see page 39).

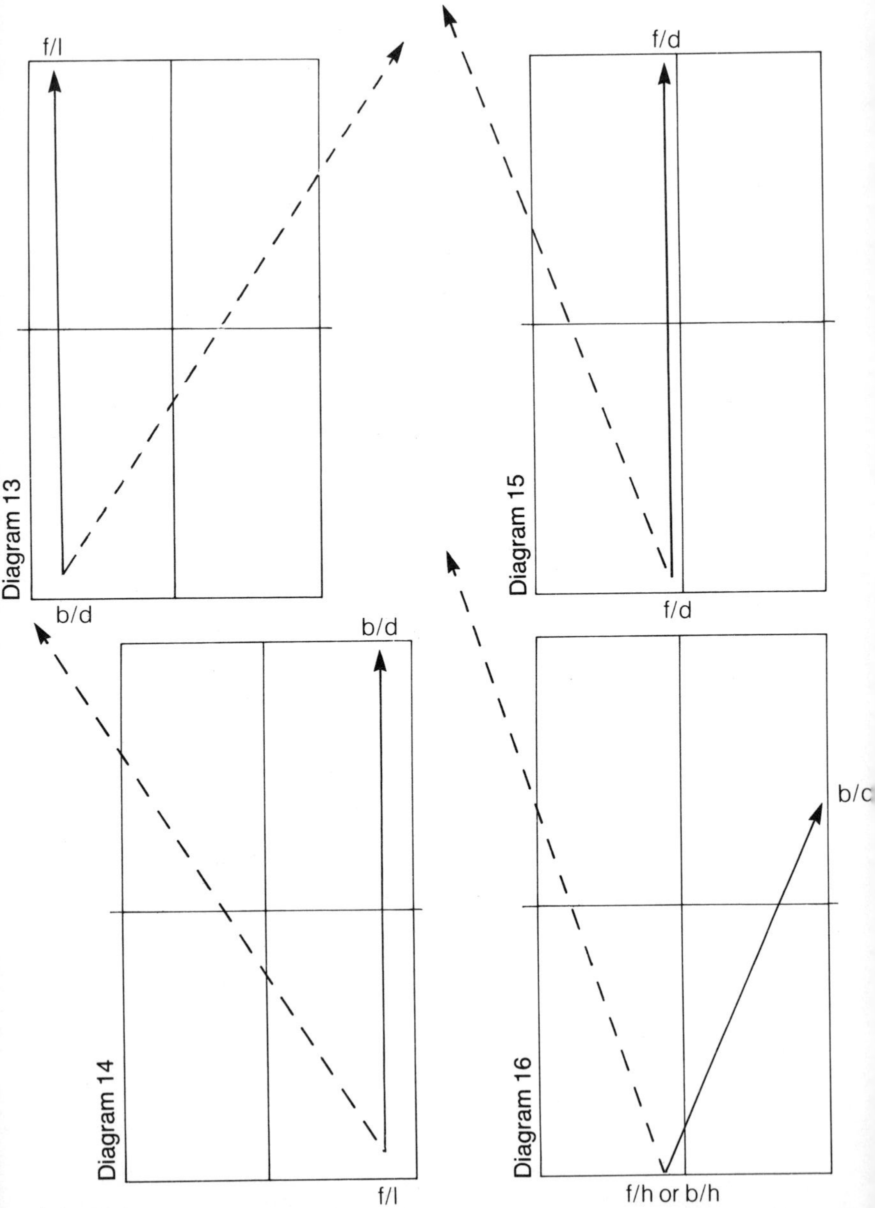

f/l
Diagram 13
b/d
f/d
Diagram 15
f/d
b/d
Diagram 14
f/l
b/c
Diagram 16
f/h or b/h

Moving away from the ball is one of the more difficult areas of movement, as you can see from our 'goalkeeper'. In his correct crouch position (right) he makes an ideal target. Diagrams 17, 18, 19 and 20 look to expose this weakness.

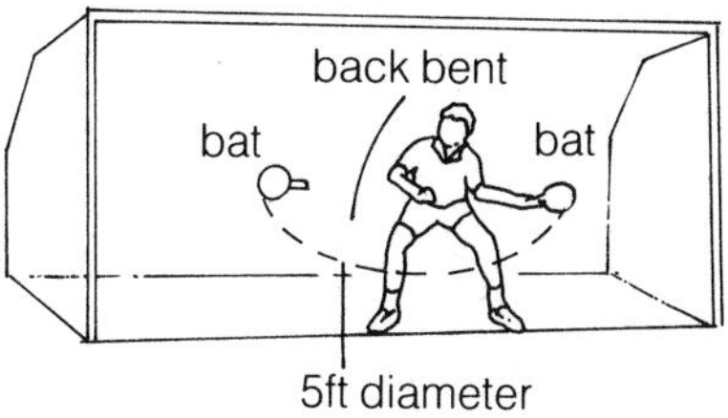

Within this range a player has good control and there are few problems. In fact, the difficulty that most players suffer from is not in moving *to* the ball but in moving *away* from the ball. This is more subtle and less natural.

One of the best ways of exposing this weakness is to play first wide and then into the body, or go wide on both wings before attacking the body (see Diagrams 17, 18, 19, 20).

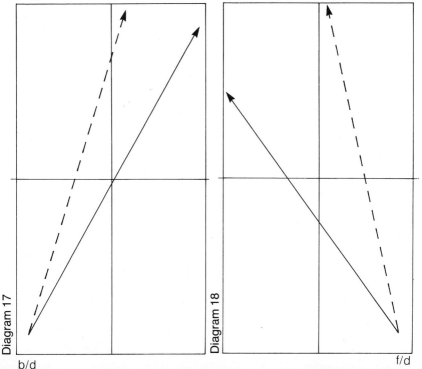

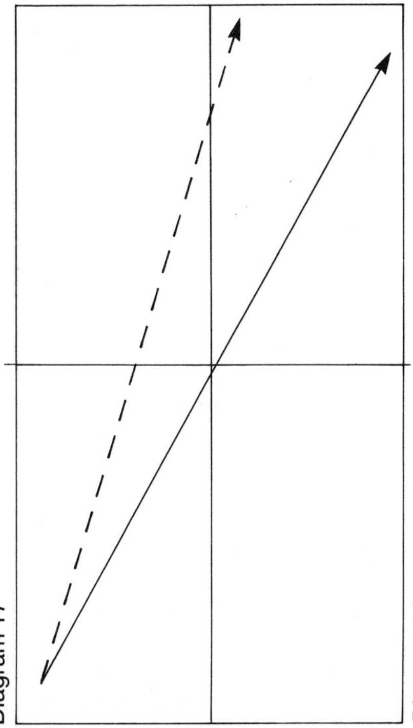

Diagram 17

b/d

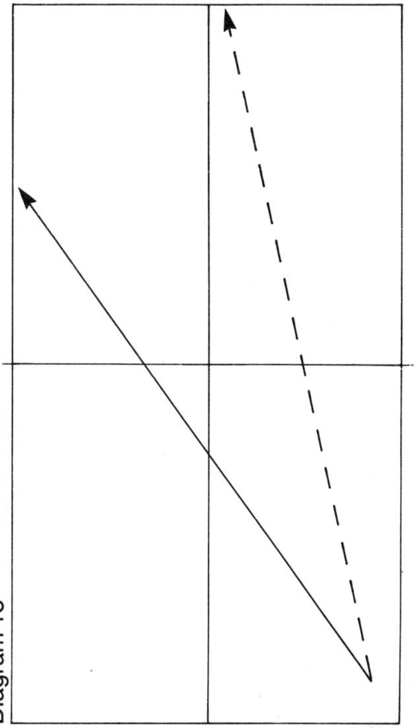

Diagram 18

f/d

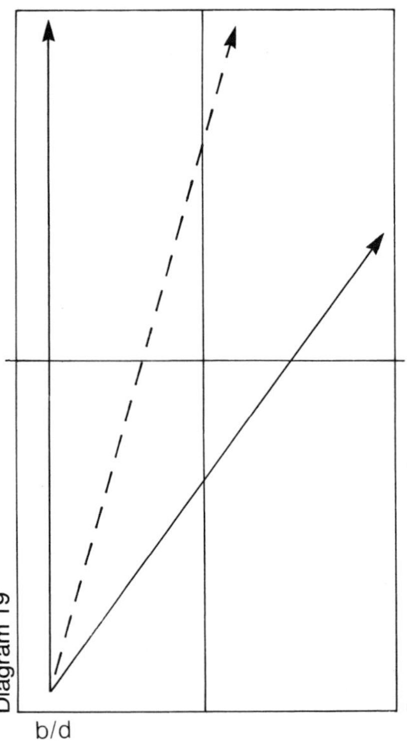

Diagram 19

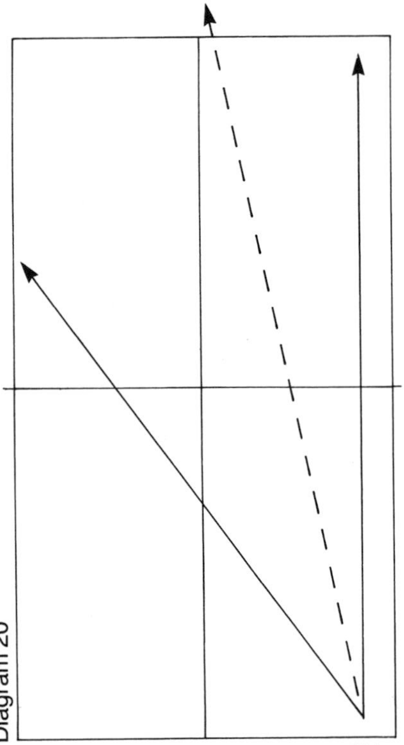

Diagram 20

The Crossover Point (X-point)

When attacking the body of your opponent the place to aim for is his *playing elbow* or his hip. Your object is to make him become indecisive – not knowing whether to play on the forehand or backhand. That moment of indecision, combined with the difficulty of playing such a ball, normally results in a weak return.

The X-point is a weak area for all players.

If you have played hard and accurately to the X-point your opponent may suffer a 'multiple reaction'.

You may have experienced this yourself where you just can't decide whether to play forehand or backhand and end up playing about six of each all in one stroke! The ball normally ends up coming off your bat at a right-angle!

Since the backhand is normally taken earlier than the forehand, this ball is most effective when played from the backhand wing (Diagram 21).

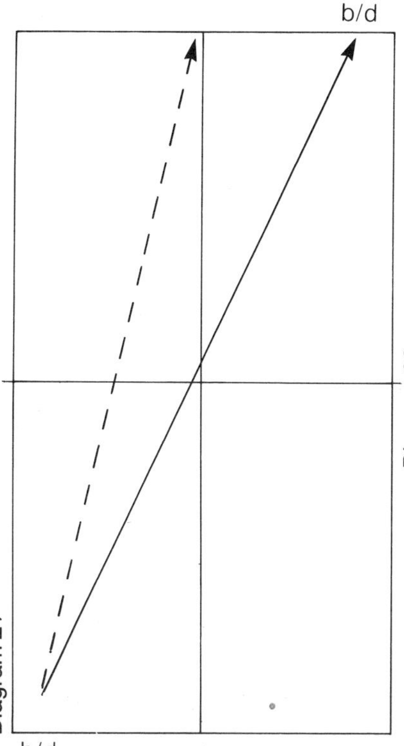

Diagram 21

From the other wing, the opponent can wait for the ball to pass across his body into his forehand (Diagram 22).

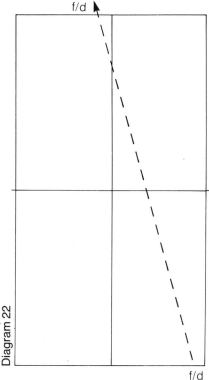

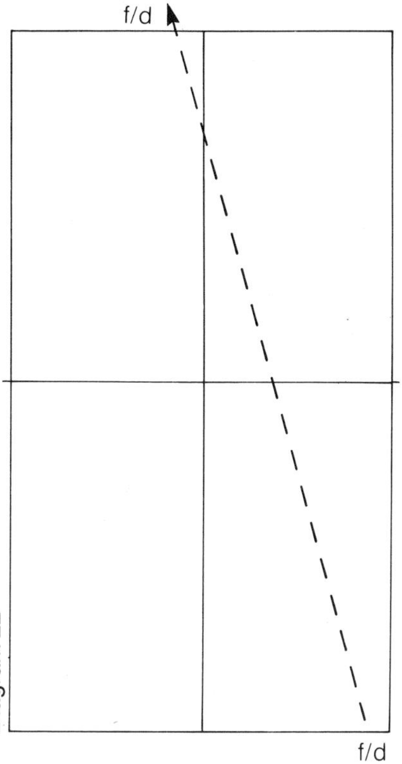

Diagram 22

Changing Direction

Table tennis is a very explosive, dynamic and sudden game. Players do not get settled into their starting blocks before they have to move. Instead, it's all about stopping, starting, changing direction, accelerating and sometimes that change is needed when your weight is completely on the wrong foot.

To wrong-foot your opponent the tactic may be to constantly change from backhand to forehand (Diagram 23) or play first to the middle, then wide to either wing and then change direction (Diagram 24).

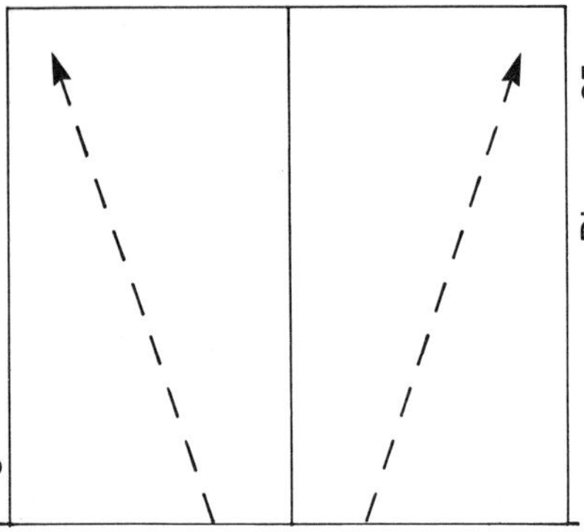

Diagram 23

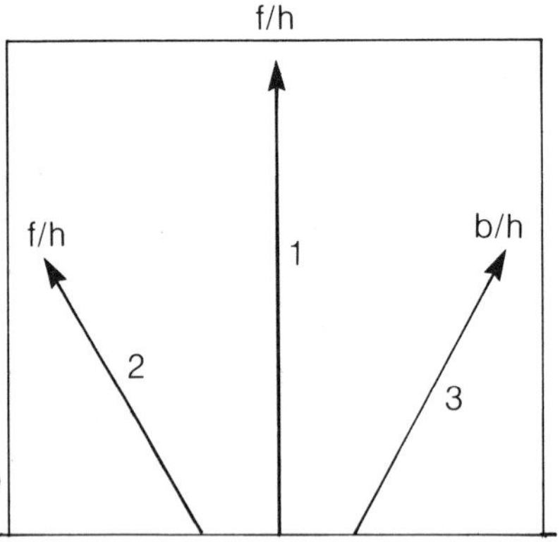

Diagram 24

A poorer tactic is to play wide, then to the X-point and then to the other wing (Diagram 25) as the player is already in motion and moving towards your next ball. It is easy to move whilst already in motion.

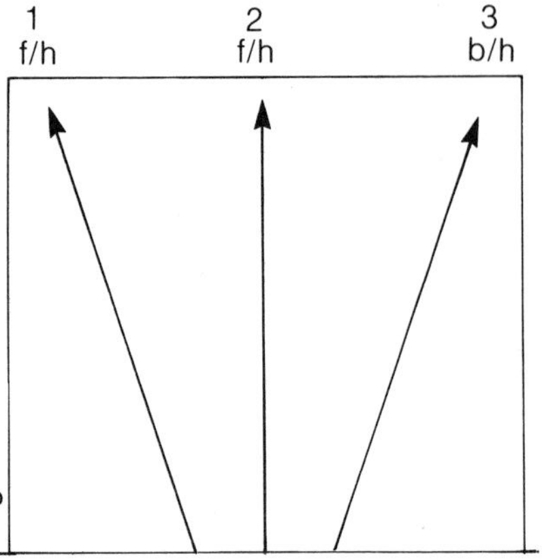

Diagram 25

Rather like when your car breaks down, once you have overcome the initial inertia and you've got it going it's easier to push.

Don't allow the other player to acquire a relaxed rhythm. Stop him flowing. By constantly moving the ball about you may help him to flow. Break him up and get him on to his heels. This can be achieved by playing a number of balls virtually to one point before changing direction (Diagram 26).

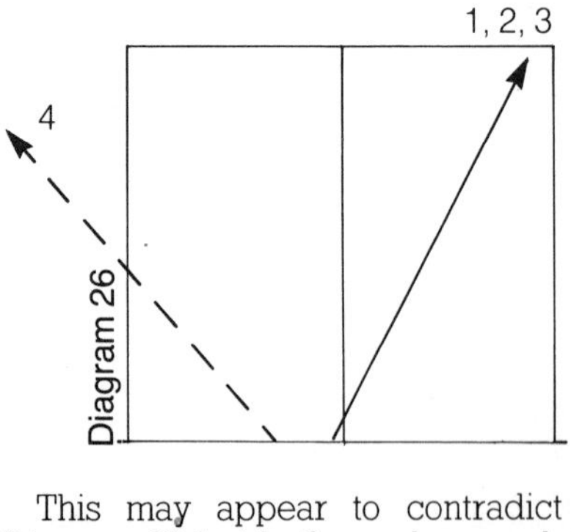

Diagram 26

This may appear to contradict Diagram 23 but both can be excellent tactics at different times. Remember that your tactics should not be predictable. It's just a case of knowing when to change from one tactical 'box' to another.

Action Whilst in Motion

Once you are already moving it can be easier to make some action than when starting from a stationary position. But there are two reasons why this may not always be the case.

The first is lack of fitness. As the other player tires the wide ball becomes an increasingly attractive option, relentlessly keeping him on the go the whole time.

You can't win just with fitness. Even if you are fit, this doesn't, of course, make your service better or your strokes spinnier. It just means that you are able to move your body more efficiently. However, if you are not fit, you may as well pack your bags, because you will soon be rooted out.

The second reason for poor movement whilst in motion is a lack of distance awareness. Often players over-compensate and end up too close to the ball, causing restrictions in stroke production.

To test your opponent out you need accurate placement. Move the ball around, just a few inches at a time, and wait for a compromising weak ball. This is a common tactic among top European players who then pounce immediately.

In practical terms this overstepping normally occurs on the forehand side where generally more movement is required. Although I would never advocate it, under pressure it is possible to compromise on the backhand and still play an effective stroke. On the forehand you always need to take up a good position to make an impact.

In and Out of the Table

This is the footwork required for defensive players and those who base their game on topspin (loop) attack. The obvious tactic tends to be the occasional short ball to encourage a slow return (Diagram 27). This is quite a good ploy but in some instances it is only half the tactic. The ball *after* the short one is the decisive strike aimed fast and long into the body (Diagram 28). When a player is moving in the same direction as the ball (ie backwards) he is most likely to be disorientated and his weight is also moving away from the table.

Diagram 27

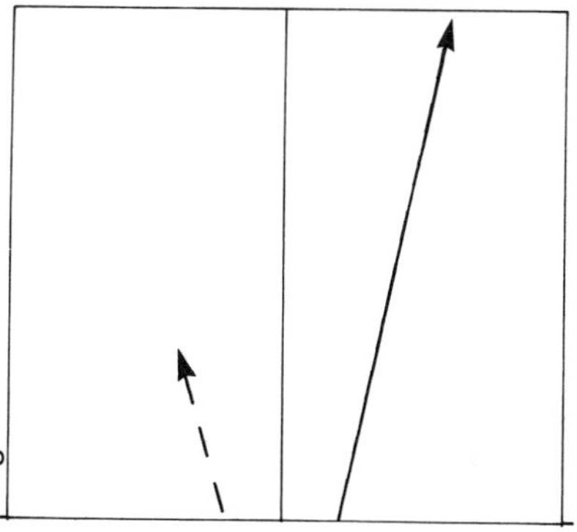

Long then short is half the tactic.

Another useful and seldom-used tactic is to bring the player in on one side of the table and take him away on the other (Diagrams 29 and 30).

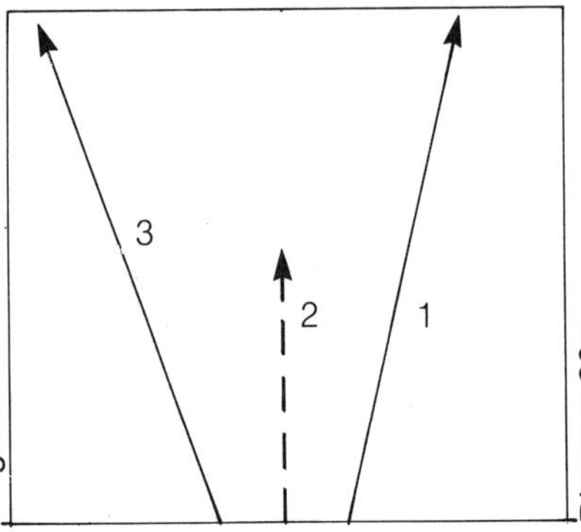

Diagram 28

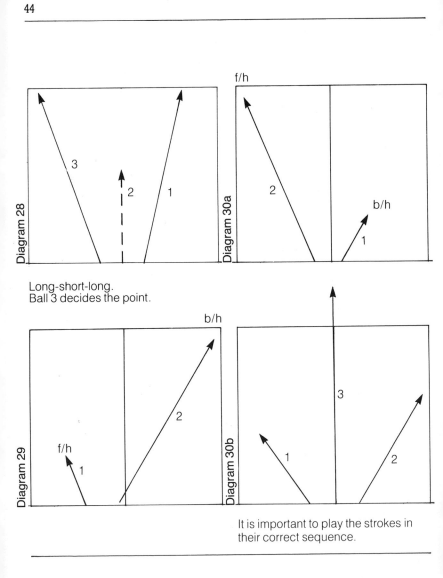

Long-short-long.
Ball 3 decides the point.

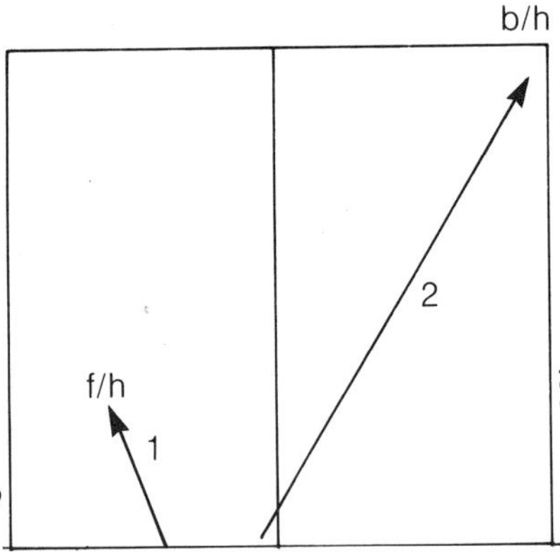

Diagram 29

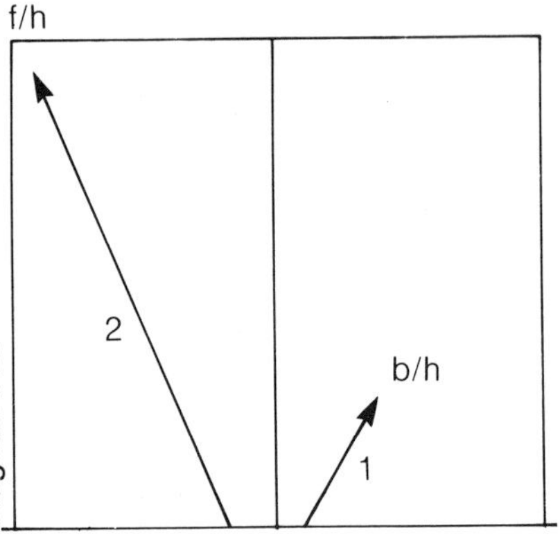

Diagram 30a

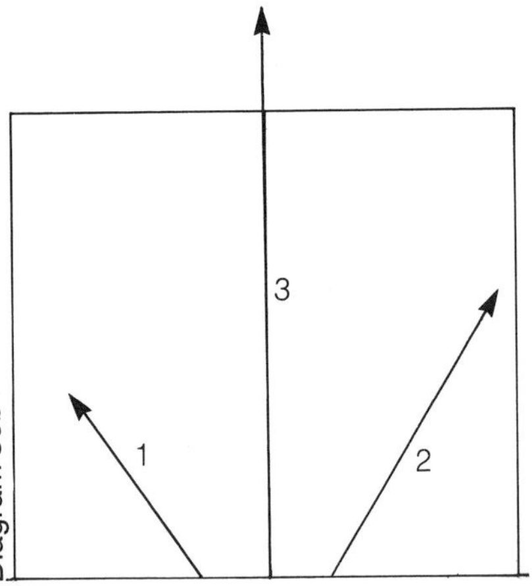

Diagram 30b

It is important to play the strokes in their correct sequence.

Service with a Snarl!

In table tennis a player often has a pre-determined plan for the whole of the forthcoming point; this is called a set piece. This will be either serve, third or fifth ball combinations, if serving, or second and fourth balls if receiving.

The Japanese, for example, tend to plan whole matches around set pieces. A serving Japanese player will expect a particular return and play a pre-determined follow-up (third ball). When receiving he may already have decided how to return the serve and play his next shot regardless.

This single-minded approach is a very decisive way of playing but it can be restricting. However, set pieces are winning tactics when they are used at the right time.

Play set pieces when they are likely to work and your opponent least expects them. Towards the end of this section there are some set piece options from service to the fifth ball of the rally.

There are many service tactics and most of them seem to be dictated by fashion.

The History of Service

Before 1950 when everybody played with pimpled bats (no sponge) the long sweeping service was favoured to drive the opponent away from the table. With the advent of sponge, maximum spin was the order of the day since most players did not understand the mechanics of spin. By the 1960s everybody had adapted to this new concept and returned service easily with a 'cushioned touch' against the spin, or else 'knocked the spin off' by attacking the ball. Other players received the ball late, allowing the spin to die.

As a result a tighter service was needed and by 1970 most players could serve well with spin, while keeping the ball short. In table tennis a short ball is defined as one which will bounce twice on the other side of the table, thus restricting the opponent's backswing and hence his choice of return.

This was highlighted in 1979 when England's Desmond Douglas played Dragutin Surbek of Yugoslavia in the European League. Desmond served the whole of his quota of services short to prevent the loop attack. He achieved this but his tactics never changed throughout the whole match and so Des eventually lost.

Disguise has always been important in service and the 1977 World Championships in England marked the advent of the combination bat. This bat has two sides of rubber giving very different levels of spin and gave the Chinese players a great advantage. They 'twiddled' the bat for service, first with the fast, spinny rubber then played the same service with the anti-spin rubber.

A good service in the 1980s utilizes all the various historical developments and spin, speed, placement, variation and deception are all part of the server's repertoire.

Top players serve just short of the middle area in order that the second bounce lands just before, just after or on the baseline. This is often called the 'half-long' service since the receiver cannot tell whether the service is long enough to loop. This makes him indecisive and forces many weak returns.

Of course good players now have a wide armoury of services, many of which have an identical backswing for maximum deception and minimum predictability.

The service is an individual skill which requires copying and developing, ingenuity and above all, practice.

Return of Service

If the service is tactically the most important stroke then the return must be a close second. A variety of returns is required to meet the ever-expanding range of service.

There are four standard returns. The secret is to ensure your preparation (backswing) is similar for all of these so you don't give away any clues.

Return 1 A short touch-push return is effective against a short serve. This prevents the server from following up with a long stroke. This return of service is well demonstrated by the Swede, Ulf Bengtsson, who is the 1984 European Champion.

Return 2 A more aggressive return from a short service is the flick. A good backhand or forehand flick can put the server on his heels (see page 17).

Return 3 All types of long service should be attacked with speed and topspin (for choppers too!) and this should be instinctive.

Return 4 This is an interesting ball which arose in the 1984 European Championships. The receiver would push (chop) the service very long and very fast with plenty of backspin, inviting the server to loop. Most players accepted this invitation whereupon the receiver would then loop-the-loop very early, brushing the very top of the ball. This sent it back very fast with topspin, catching the opponent cold on his loop's follow-through.

This is a risky tactic that was used mainly against the better services, but as the SAS motto goes, 'Who dares wins'.

Third, Fourth and Fifth Ball Attack

The service is the first ball of the rally and the return is the second. To continue the rally you must then deal with the third ball, ie the server's follow-up stroke.

Most players serve to enable a forehand loop or smash to follow. This is impossible if the return is short and low and easiest when the ball is returned long and slow. Such players therefore try to avoid serving either long or very short, concentrating mainly on the half-long service. This encourages a longer return without great speed. The server can then cover most of the table with a forehand loop or smash as his third ball attack. Normally this is most effective when played to the X-point (Diagram 31), but if the return is wide and not too long, a greater angle can be achieved (Diagram 32). In this case a wide attack is more useful.

If the return is short the usual third ball is to flick hard to the angles (Diagram 33).

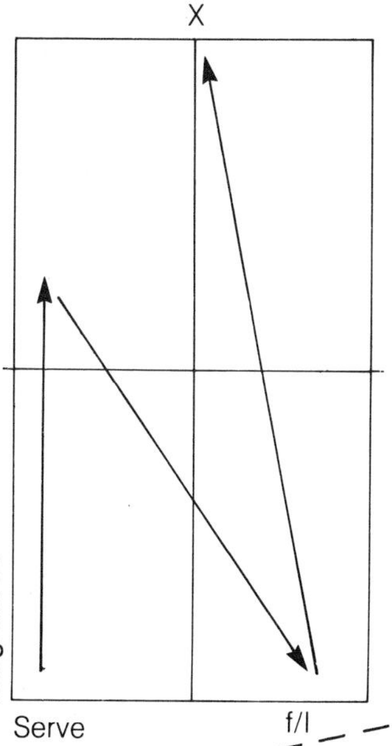

Diagram 31

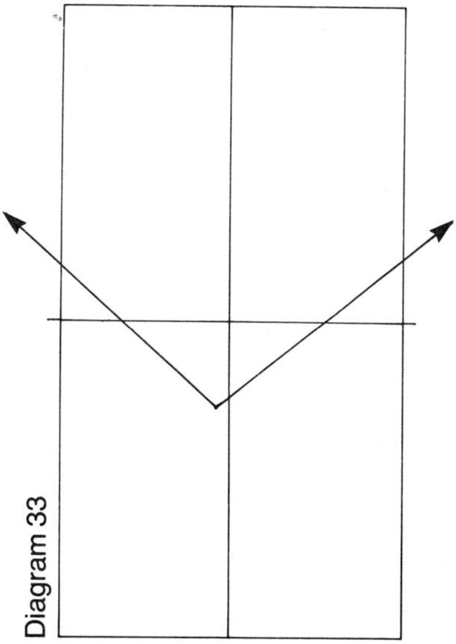

Diagram 33

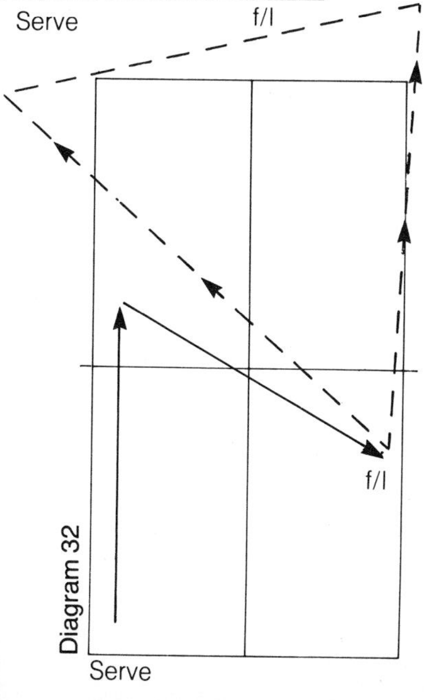

Diagram 32

Fourth Ball

It follows that the ball is usually long by this stage, so that the receiver can loop the fourth ball. If the third ball is weak it is certainly best to loop or drive this ball, but if the third ball is strong then the best tactic is to block or chop. A sensible blocked or chopped fourth ball is often the switch, buying a little time to settle into the rally.

Fifth Ball Attack

In top-class table tennis, nearly half the points are decided by the fifth ball, which is increasingly becoming the point winner. If the server cannot win the point directly from service or third ball, he normally tries to place his third ball well enough to force a weak chop or block.

Statistics show that if the server hasn't won the point after the fifth ball he is the underdog for the remainder of the rally.

Never Refuse a Backhander!

There is a recent innovation in attacking play. Ever since I have been involved in the sport it has been a cardinal sin to play a backhand attack from the forehand side, whilst forehands from the backhand side are encouraged. The received wisdom has been that such a move leaves too large a gap down the backhand side, which is normally weaker anyway (Diagram 34).

However, it is always good to see and hear something new and two of Europe's best players, Mazunov (USSR) and Grubba (Poland), use this to great advantage. They both have outstanding backhand loops and both like to play the second or third balls with the backhand. Once in the centre of the table they are

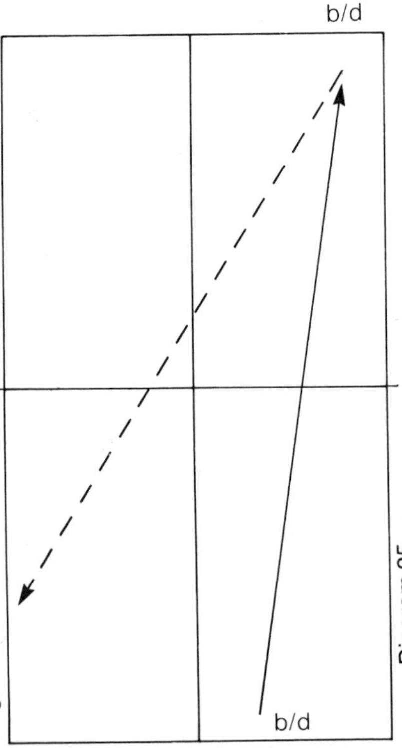

Diagram 34

Too exposed on the backhand.

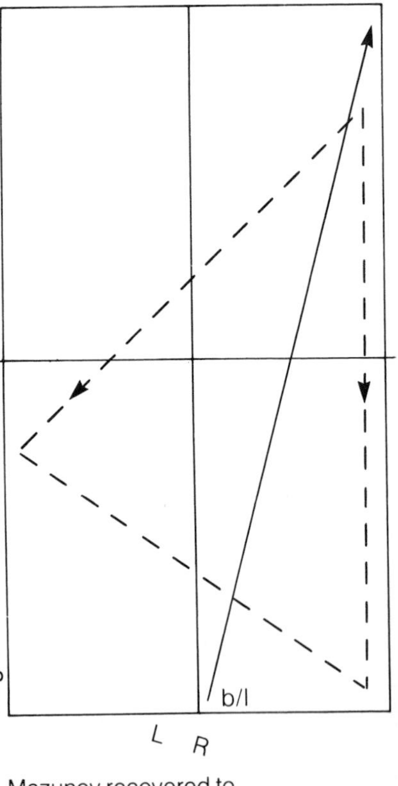

Diagram 35

Mazunov recovered to here to cover the angles

Andrez Grubba from Poland is currently the finest European player. Here he is seeking to gain a tactical advantage from his serve.

England's Carl Prean, 1985 European Junior Top Twelve winner, taking a short ball with good balance – and making excellent use of his non-playing arm.

Andrez Grubba, one of the world's most entertaining players, in a text-book ready position.

Here, Milan Orlowski from Czechoslovakia illustrates sound technique in a high-toss service.

happy to remain there for the whole rally. Again they understand the angles of play perfectly, using them to restrict the opponent's angle by playing diagonally (Diagrams 35 and 36).

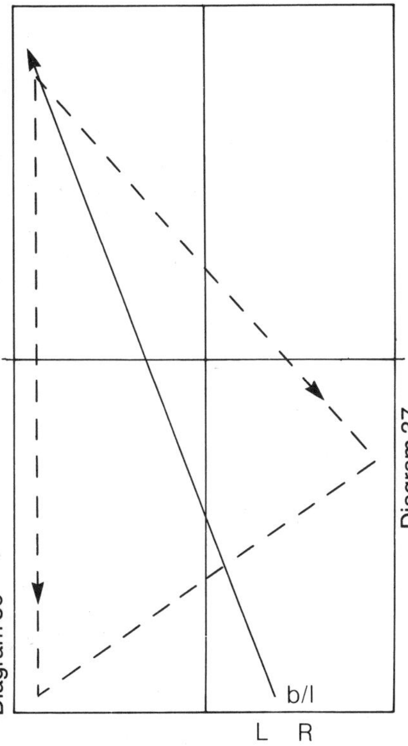

Diagram 36

Grubba's feet return here to cover the angles

They accept that a backhand loop from the forehand side must be a winner if played down the line (Diagram 37).

I feel it's better but not essential

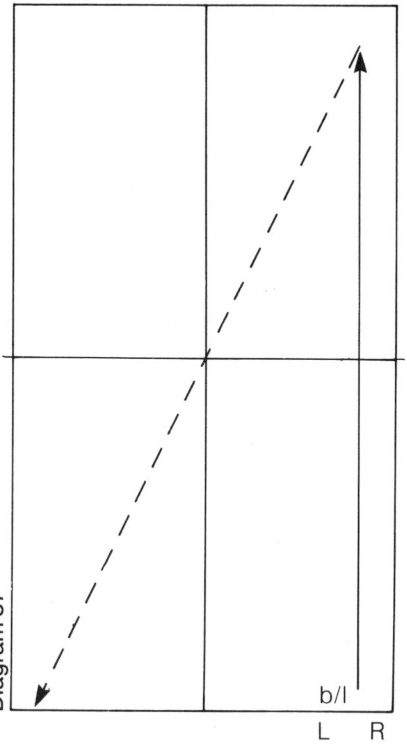

Diagram 37

Line ball puts Grubba out of position for a switched return.

to develop a backhand service to complement the backhand loop as you are then more able to prepare for a strong backhand third ball. The complexity of footwork and the time factor mean that I would only recommend a backhand loop from the *backhand* side when the service is with the forehand.

Doubles is a team game. Note Karen Witt's (England) excellent ready position and Jill Hammersley-Parker (England) bringing her eyes down to the level of the ball.

5
JAQUES

Useful Set Piece Practices

3rd Ball Set Pieces

A	B	C	D
1 Backhand serve short anywhere	1 B/serve short anywhere	1 B/serve long anywhere	1 B/serve short or long
2 Return to b/h	2 Return to f/h	2 Return either side	2 Return to X-over
3 Attack to X-over	3 Attack to X-over	3 Attack to X-over	3 Attack to X-over

Same as above but f/serve. Returns to be flicked or pushed depending on the practice requirements

5th Ball Set Pieces

1 Forehand serve short random	1 F/serve long random	1 F/serve random	1 F/serve random
2 Return to X-over	2 Return to b/h	2 Return to b/h	2 Return to f/h
3 F/attack to X-over	3 Attack to b/h	3 Attack to f/h	3 F/attack to diagonal
4 Block to f/h diagonal	4 Block to X-over	4 F/h to diagonal	4 F/block to diagonal
5 F/kill to diagonal	5 F/kill to X-over	5 F/kill to X-over	5 F/kill to X-over

Same as above but b/serve. Returns to be flicked or pushed depending on the practice requirements.

4th Ball Set Pieces

1 F/serve to f/h	1 F/serve to b/h	1 F/serve to f/h	1 F/serve to f/h
2 F/push to diagonal	2 B/push to X-over	2 F/push to diagonal	2 Long push to X-over
3 F/push to diagonal	3 Push to X-over	3 F/attack to diagonal	3 Long push to X-over
4 F/attack to X-over	4 Attack to X-over	4 F/attack to diagonal	4 F/kill to X-over

Same as above but b/serve.

E	F	G	H
1 B/serve to b/h	1 B/serve to diagonal	1 B/serve to f/h	1 B/serve short to f/h
2 B/flick to diagonal	2 B/flick to diagonal	2 F/flick to X-over	2 F/flick to diagonal
3 B/attack to diagonal	3 B/attack to diagonal	3 F/attack to diagonal	3 F/attack to diagonal
4 B/attack to X-over	4 B/attack to line	4 F/attack to diagonal	4 F/attack to X-over

Same as above but f/serve.
Attack=spin or speed or if the ball is right – kill.

Your Opponent and His Game

Having discussed tactics that are used against any player we now consider that every table tennis player has his or her individual game. No two players play alike. Most players, though, can be categorized into one or more broad groups, such as serve and loopers, blockers, choppers, slow players, forehand-biased, pen-grip, left-handers and so on, ad infinitum. Naturally it is important to understand the strengths and weaknesses of these different groups.

It is no use, however, if by the time you discover your opponent's strengths and weaknesses, you are already heading for defeat. So you must always find out about your opponent before the match and during the first game. Once you understand your opponent, you can choose which tactics to employ.

The best way to learn about opponents is to watch them play. Talking about opponents without seeing them in action is often not really helpful, because the information is second-hand and it is easy to build a false image.

It amazes me how some players set about studying their opponents. At tournaments you may see players standing alongside the court, level with the net, or else at the top of the tiered seating! This positioning gives the following view (below).

When you are actually in play, your view of the opponent is head-on and this is therefore the best position for studying your opponent (see page 54).

If possible, watch your opponent play against someone who has a similar style to your own. Then you can mentally place yourself on court, copying, surprising and dominating your opponent.

Look for all tell-tale signs that will help your anticipation, particularly the *elbow* which gives cues to the speed and direction of the ball. You will also learn subconsciously, pic-

Good for spectating but not the best position to learn about your opponent.

Excellent position to view your next opponent.

king up pieces of information which will build up into a complete picture of your adversary. Your coach may also spot weaknesses and predictability by using the analysis chart given on page 26.

There is a certain type of player who gives his opponent much too much respect. If you are in this category I would recommend that you do not concern yourself too much with studying your opponent! It may be that you will achieve better results by expressing yourself naturally without the restrictions of different tactical thinking for different opponents. Just use your general tactics and play independently of the person at the other end, unless something becomes obvious as the match progresses. Keep to *your* style of play, improvise under pressure and you will keep your natural rhythm and flow.

Most players however can feed on any information gained about the opponent and can use this to their advantage.

Early in the first game you should learn about your opponent's play by varying your services and returns and finding out how hard to attack in the rallies.

His strengths will then become clearer and his weaknesses will either appear or he will hide them. Either way, you know how to probe his most sensitive areas! Once you know what to expect you can plan your attack.

Tactics Against Particular Styles

There are probably more distinct styles of player in table tennis than in any other sport. You need to learn how to combat a great variety of styles – a good player cannot excuse himself by saying 'I can't play against left-handers'.

The main styles of play you are likely to be faced with are:

The left-handed player.
The penholder.
The chopper.
The combination bat player.
The blocker.
The looper.

Left-Handers

One in ten people are born left-handed. All things being equal then, there should be only one left-hander in England's Top Ten table tennis players. However, in 1985 for instance, there were six left-handers near the top of the men's list. This is not an unusual year either as proportionately left-handers have always dominated the sport.

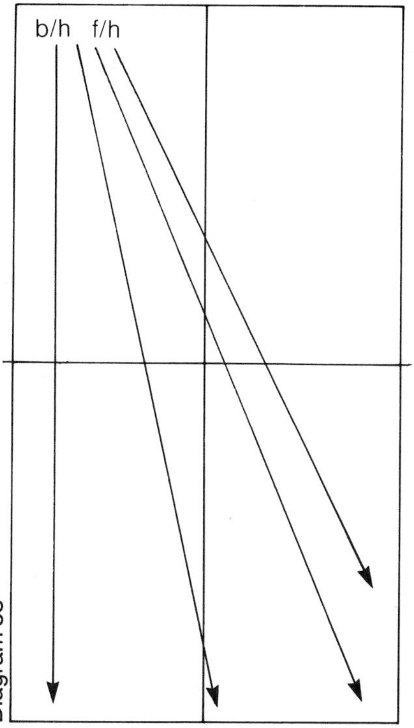

Diagram 38

Some would argue that the reason for this dominance is that left-handers have a better ability to solve spatial problems and are better able to judge angles and see things in reverse – and therefore to receive and place awkward shots.

Whatever the reasons, the 'leftie' generally seems to be well-balanced and technically sound. My message to coaches is 'treasure your lefties', they are your jewels! The problem with left-handers is how to beat them! By tradition they have strong forehands and weaker backhands, and the usual tactic tends to be to drive the ball into the backhand for security (see Diagram 38). This is usually a bad tactic because:

They are used to it.

They have learned to protect it skilfully.

Out of necessity they have a superb forehand game from the backhand side of the table.

From Diagram 39 you can see how to overcome this problem. Lefties often leave open spaces on their forehand wing so a strong ball wide to a left-hander's forehand normally results in a half-attack. This ball can *then* be played into the backhand,

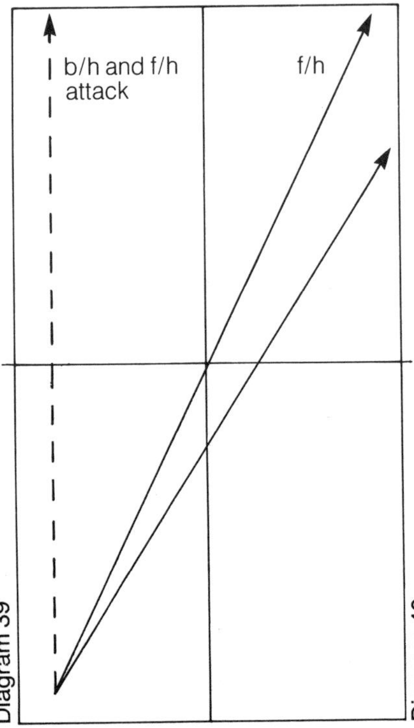

Diagram 39

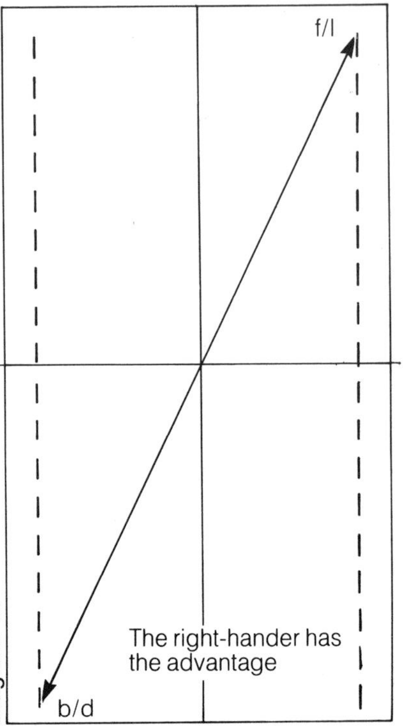

Diagram 40

exposing their weakness.

As in the tactics of switching (see page 31), remember you are the right-hander playing backhands diagonally to the forehand. You have the more effective switch ball into his backhand in this confrontation (Diagram 40).

The right-hander has the advantage of variation, recovery and unpredictability so the switch into the weakness can be very rewarding.

The key for left-handers is to play a good line ball with the forehand and recover towards the backhand (Diagram 41).

Penholders

Ever since the Orientals began producing pen-grip players, coaches have instructed players to play the penholder on the backhand. As with the left-hander the backhand is considered a weaker stroke, and the forehand regarded as a serious threat.

However, the tactic of pinning the penholder on the backhand is even greater folly than with the left-hander. It is second nature for the pen-grip player to play forehands from the backhand side since he is normally fast on his feet to avoid too

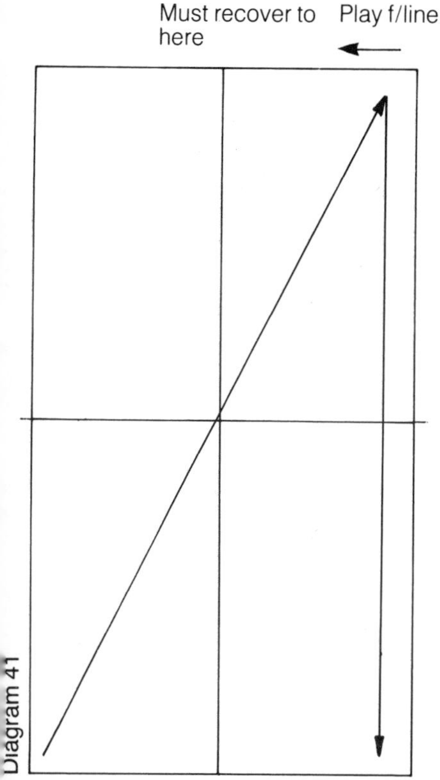

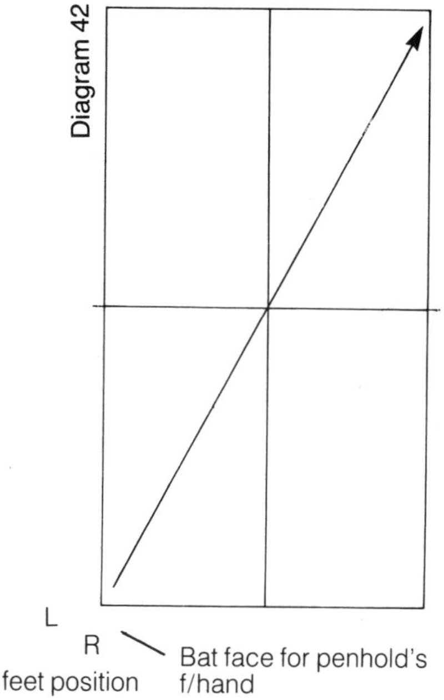

much backhand play. The grip itself also encourages this tactic since the bat angle will naturally face the opposite diagonal (Diagram 42).

The tactics now become like a game of chess, with the penholder's backhand as the King. It is difficult to expose the King since it is well protected and he has bunched his best pieces around it. The only way to bring him out of cover is to play *wide* to the forehand. The key ball is now the penholder's forehand attack. If it is good, he wins the point. If it is poor it is 'checkmate' on the exposed backhand. The move for the pen-grip player is to attack this ball across the diagonal as accurately as possible (Diagram 43). This cuts down the angle into the King.

Choppers

Playing against chop is tactically one of the most difficult games *if you are evenly matched*. It is more important to skip from one tactical 'box' to another than when playing against any other style of opponent.

Nearly all defenders rely on rhythm. Firstly they get *themselves* into a rhythm and then they get *you* into *their* rhythm. When this situa-

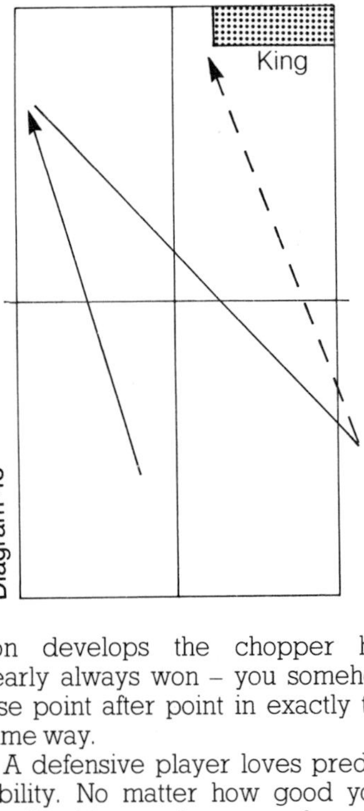

Diagram 43

tion develops the chopper has nearly always won – you somehow lose point after point in exactly the same way.

A defensive player loves predictability. No matter how good your predictable tactics are, he will eventually overcome them:

1. If your predictable tactic is to loop and drop shot, you will find the chopper gliding in and out while you play too short (into the net) and too long (off the end).
2. If your predictable tactic is to drive or loop patiently you will make a mistake before he does.
3. If your predictable tactic is to attack the third and fifth balls hard, you will miss more often than you hit winners.
4. If your predictable tactic is to play as slowly as he does, you will suffer the indignity of being 'hit off' by a defender.

Variation is the answer. Although predictable tactics are all excellent when used in combination, they are ineffective when used alone. The secret is to choose the right tactical box for the particular defender. Adopt this tactic for about 70% of the game but, each time you feel that your opponent is starting to play in a rhythm (or if you are!), change your tactics. Even if it is for only one point and (dare I say it) even if you lose that point your defensive adversary can never be sure what to expect.

Combination Bat Players

With the introduction of the Colour Code early in 1984, the combination bat doesn't pose quite the problems it used to. At least you can now see which side of the bat has struck the ball and can analyse the effect immediately.

Every standard bat player will nevertheless tell you that it's difficult and messy to play against the combi-bat as the pace and spin constantly alter with the different surfaces.

There are really three main tactics against the 'funny bat'. The first is easy to describe but far harder to execute; that is to drive your adversary away from the table. Having achieved this the effects of the combination are reduced as the spin dies over time, and you have longer to examine the bat and ball. The aggressive combi-bat player will also be less intimidating from a distance.

Secondly we know that both 'long pimples' and 'anti-spin' are *parasite* rubbers. They gain their effects by feeding off the spin imparted by the opponent.

By merely hitting hard and with spin you are playing into the hands of the enemy as he uses your own spin against you. Give the parasite side nothing and he will have nothing to play with. For example long services with no spin or long slow 'rolls' are difficult to bite into

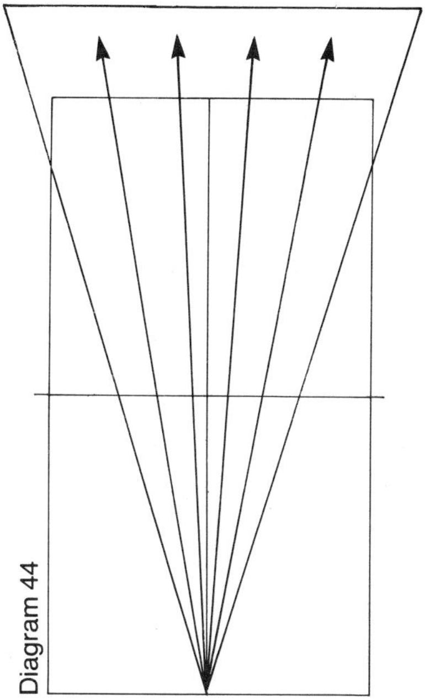

Diagram 44

Long balls mean less threatening returns.

with a combi-bat (Diagram 44).

Putting two tactics together, first drive the combination player away from the table and then, giving him little or no spin, play a little shorter. You will then receive a 'nothing ball' which you can attack *hard* while he

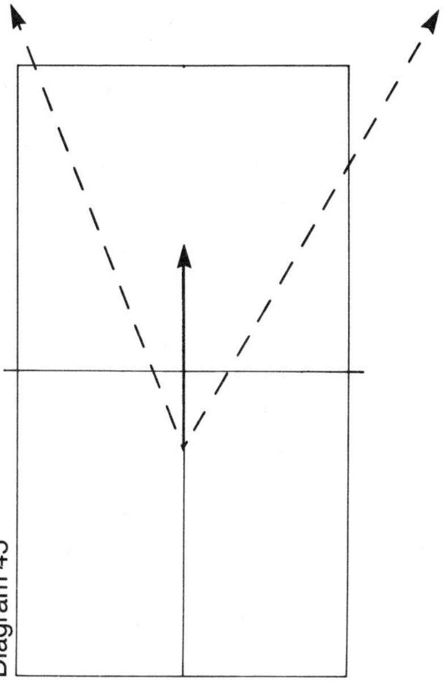

Diagram 45

Slightly shorter ball with less spin – follow with penetrating attack.

is running backwards (Diagram 45).

The third tactic that has been successful against the combi-bat is to seek out the 'funny' side with a fast, heavy push or chop. The return will almost always be the opposite spin (ie topspin) which you can attack with as much power as possible (Diagram 46).

Blockers

Blockers will nearly always be very

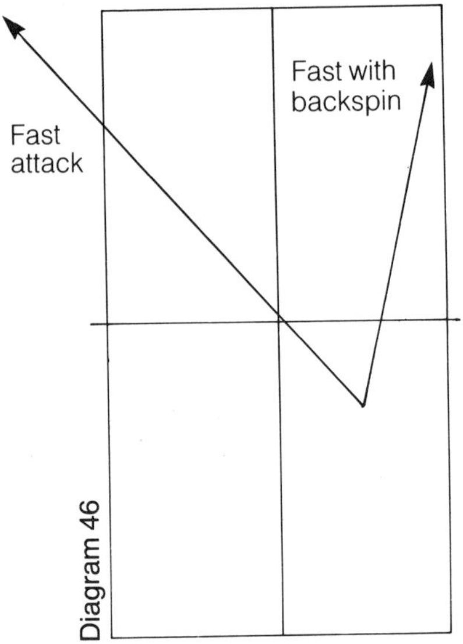

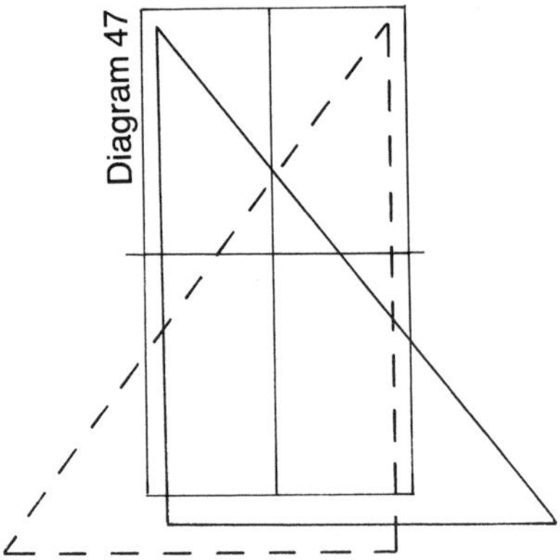

By playing wide you create angles for the blocker.

consistent and play the angles like a geometry teacher! To combat the blocker you need firstly to be very fit as you are undoubtedly in for a long game. Secondly your footwork will be put to the test as he constantly tries to out-manoeuvre you.

The important point is that the blocker can only *mirror* your speed. Play slowly and he will return slowly, play fast and you will have fast balls coming back. Likewise, by giving him angled balls you are giving angled opportunities to the blocker (Diagram 47).

It follows that a good tactic is to spin the ball high and deep to the middle, reducing his angle of vision and giving him no pace to feed off. After a number of these balls play a quick switch to either angle, surprising the blocker (Diagrams 48, 49).

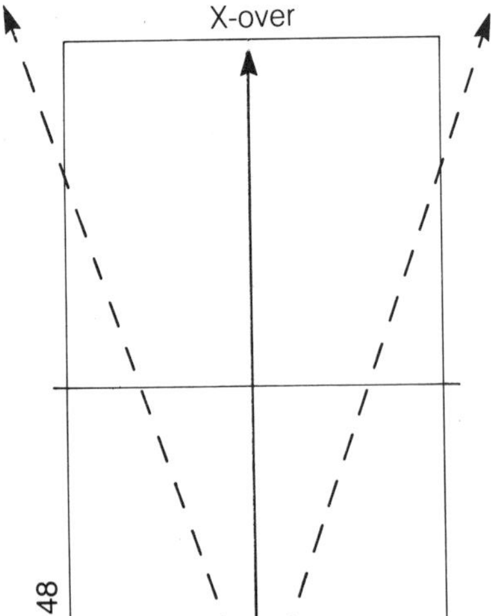

Brute force and ignorance are useless against the blocker.

Diagram 49

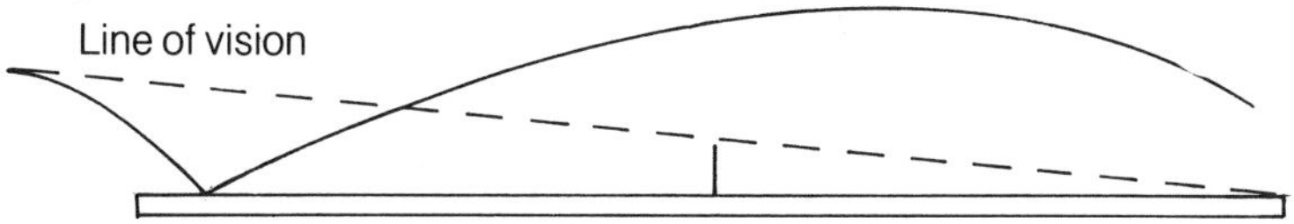

Long ball cuts the angle of vision resulting in a safe return.

Diagram 50

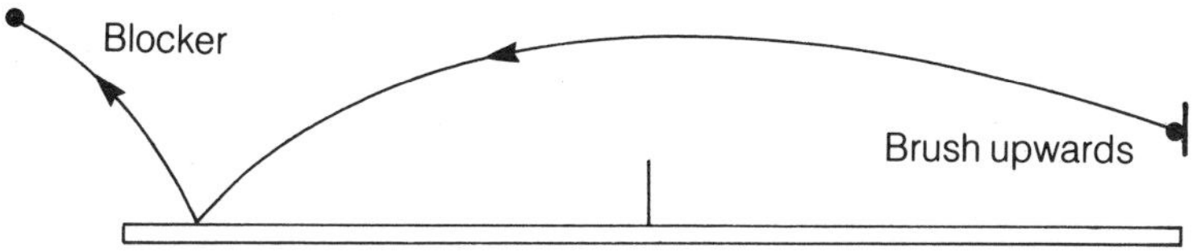

Brush the back of the ball upwards to produce a slow, spinny loop (Diagram 50).

Diagram 51

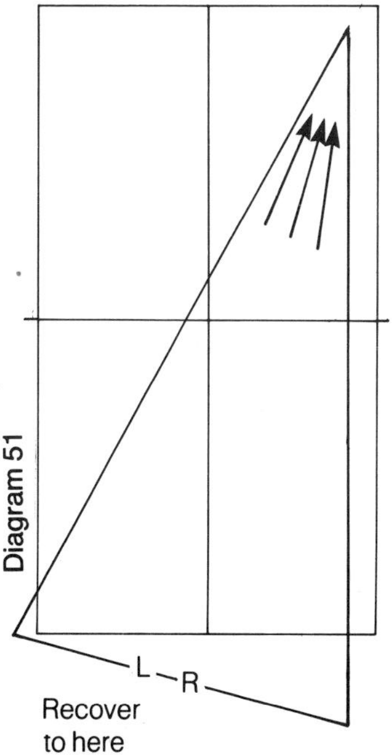

A good alternative tactic is to attack solely to one corner (Diagram 51). This limits the blocker's range of angle so that you know exactly where to recover after every stroke. When you see the opportunity arise, punish the looser ball to the X-point (Diagram 52).

The blocker needs to obey some simple rules to combat these tactics. By nature the blocker is master of the switch and he should remember to block down the line when in trouble. This is more awkward for the attacking player and gives him less time to recover for his next stroke. In the 'comfortable' rally

Diagram 52

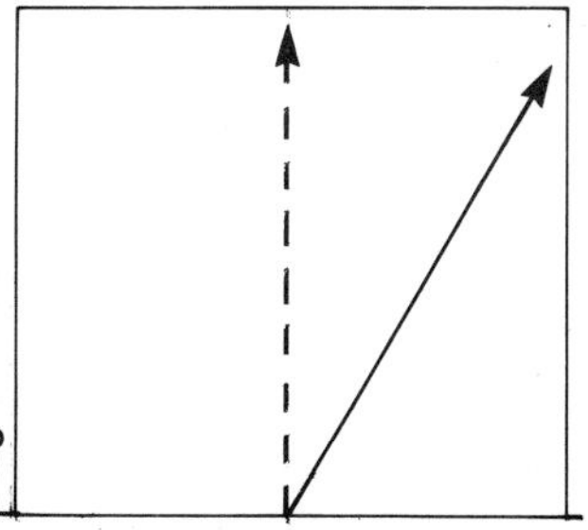

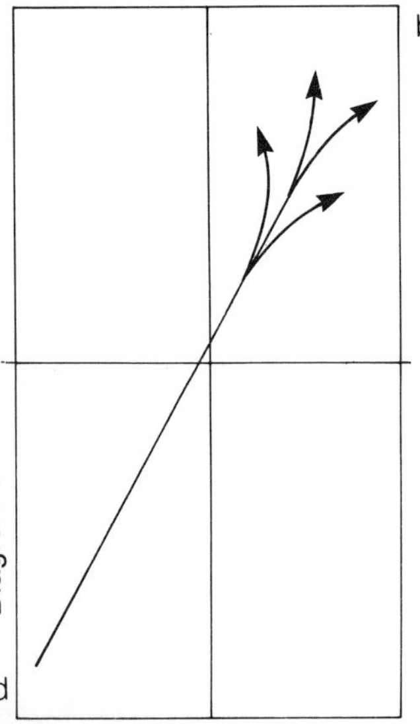

Diagram 53

play try to pin your enemy on the backhand diagonal (Diagram 53). You can then use your superior counter-hits to make the small, delicate switches without detection.

As the better switching and angle player it obviously helps to create bigger angles for yourself. This can often be achieved by realizing that most players naturally hit drives, chops and loops a fixed distance. If you block short the ball will come back long, and if you block long your opponent will move away a little and hence play a shorter ball back (Diagram 54).

When you receive this shorter ball the angles are greatly widened (Diagrams 55 and 56).

By playing long you also drive your enemy away from the table where it is dangerous to play slowly. You can then feed off his pace with plenty of angle.

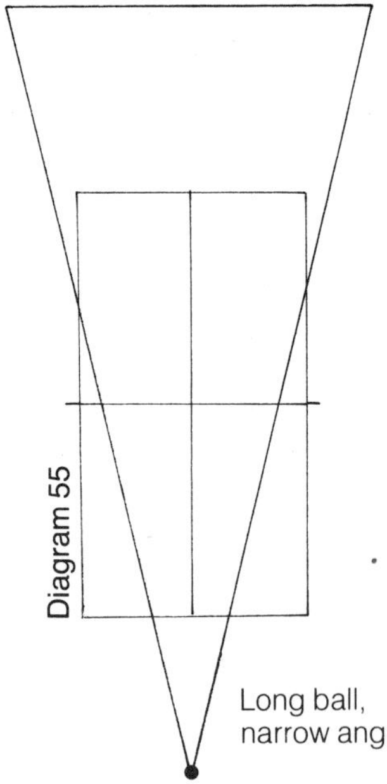

Diagram 55

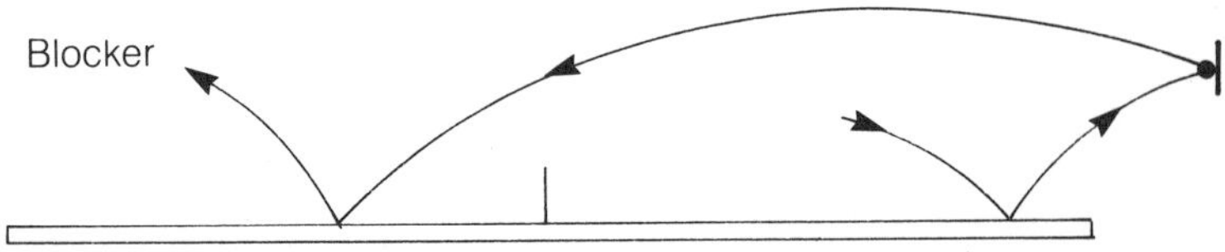

Diagram 54

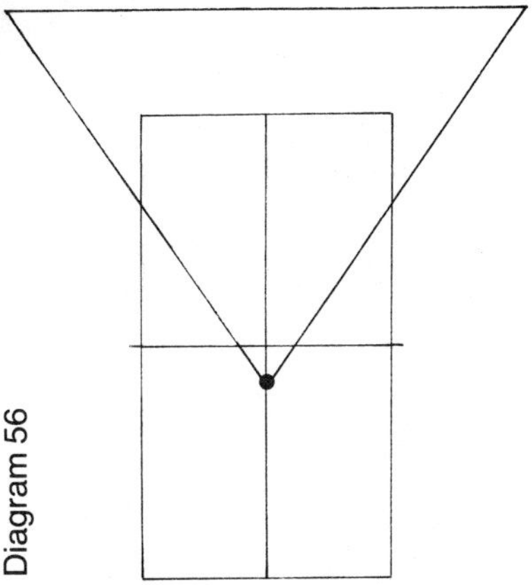

Diagram 56

Short balls for greater angles

Loopers

A table tennis ball is difficult to control in simple play, and a heavily spun ball rotating at 2000 rpm can be a real headache. The problems multiply with the different trajectories caused by the variations of 12 o'clock, 9 o'clock and intermediate looping (Diagram 57).

It is easier to topspin a slow ball since you have longer to 'eye-up' the ball (for good timing). It is also easier to topspin a backspin ball because it is rotating the same way before and after your stroke (Diagram 58).

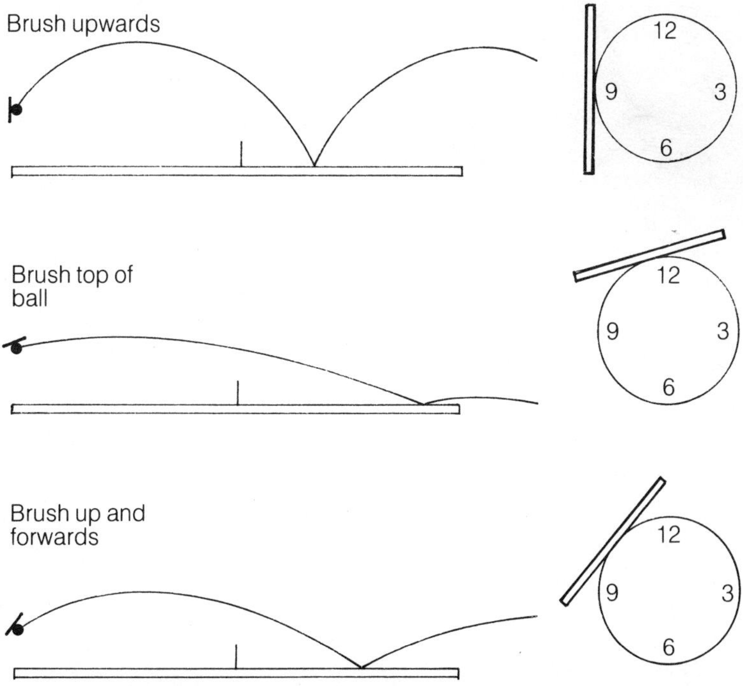

Diagram 57

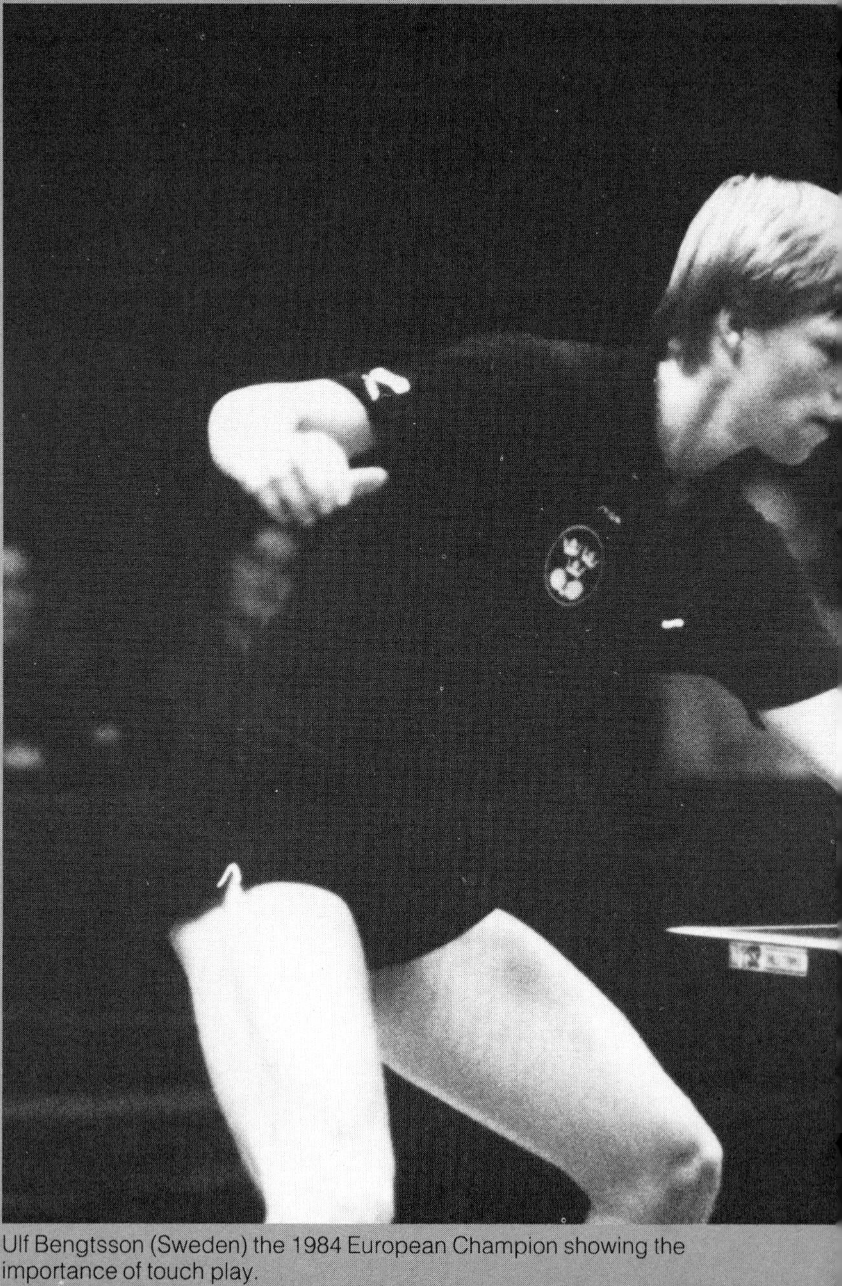

Ulf Bengtsson (Sweden) the 1984 European Champion showing the importance of touch play.

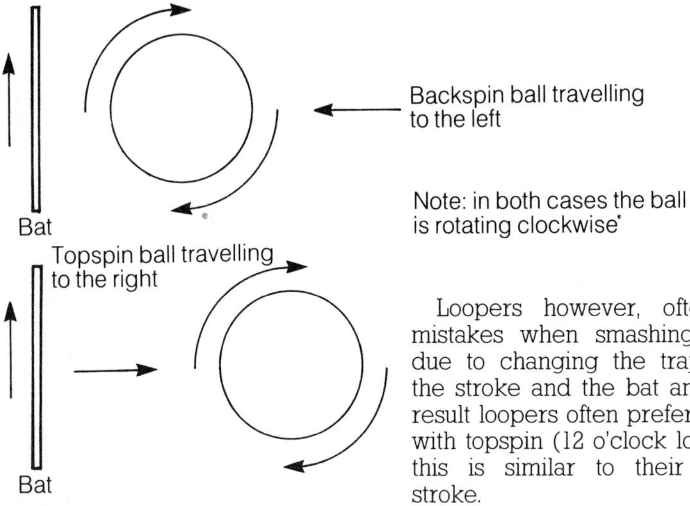

Diagram 58

It follows that you are looking for a long push to loop. As such it is vital to serve and receive serve well to force a long push from your adversary as early in the rally as possible.

A good half-long serve with chop will often result in a long push or chop return which you can loop effectively. When receiving, a short push return will often force the enemy to push long. Then your 'fourth ball loop' will come into play.

Once you have the opportunity to loop it is usually best to aim to the forehand or X-point, because the blocking of loops is easiest with the backhand. A fast loop may win the point outright (but will return quicker if not). A slow loop with heavy topspin is more likely to give you a high ball next, but it is easier to attack. Good judgement in your speed of loop will win points directly or give you the ball to smash.

Loopers however, often make mistakes when smashing. This is due to changing the trajectory of the stroke and the bat angle. As a result loopers often prefer to smash with topspin (12 o'clock loop) since this is similar to their previous stroke.

The looper is nevertheless vulnerable. Generally loop strokes are long, making recovery difficult and timing has to be spot-on every time as there is little margin for error. It is also difficult to spin a ball that has pace.

Playing against loop normally requires plenty of speed to reduce the spin on the loop.

Backspin players should use the fast *float* ball. The long chop should be avoided if at all possible – push short or flick when the looper is looking for his favourite ball.

More switching than usual will highlight the problems that the looper has in recovery and will upset his rhythm. Do not be afraid to play rallies with the looper. His timing needs to be exact and it requires a great deal of effort to produce one single loop. All other things being equal you should win the fitness stakes and the match.

Doubles Play

Doubles is a very important part of table tennis with doubles events in nearly all tournaments and often in local league play. At a higher level doubles play becomes a vital skill. For instance, in the European League two out of seven sets are doubles.

In international team events the women always (and the men sometimes) play under the Corbillon Cup system.

The Corbillon Cup System

Team 1	*Team 2*
Player A	Player X
Player B	Player Y

Match No. 1. A *v* X
2. B *v* Y
3. A/B *v* X/Y Doubles
4. A *v* Y
5. B *v* X

When one team has amassed three victories the match is over, and note that there will always be a doubles match no matter whether the result is 3-0, 3-1 or 3-2.

If the doubles is won, a team needs two other victories (probably against the opposing No. 2 player). If the doubles is lost a team needs three out of four singles wins, so that the opposing No. 1 player *must* be beaten, and probably two victories are required against the No. 2 player. The doubles is therefore the key match in the popular Corbillon Cup system.

The Complication of Doubles

Doubles matches are tactically extremely complex and I don't think anyone can honestly claim to understand doubles tactics fully. First of all there are eight different battles, which I show by way of an example.

Players A and C play against B and D. A and C win the toss and A serves. B elects to receive. After five points A and C change positions and B serves to C. After another five points B and D change places and C serves to D and so on. After 20 points the sequence has gone full circle.

By the time a pattern of tactics emerges the game is over! Worse still, in the 2nd game the order changes from A → B → C → D to D → C → B → A!

If the match goes to one game all, the third game is A → B → C → D until a pair has 10 points and then D → C → B → A for the completion of the match.

The most important thing to do is to watch your opposing pair as described on page 53. Normally you can pick out the weaker player by doing this. In mixed doubles this is usually the woman (sorry, ladies).

When you then play this pair it is vital to choose the *bad* order first. Usually this is when their stronger player plays to your weaker player. If you win the toss you can choose the order by opting to receive. They must elect a server and you choose who receives accordingly.

The reason for choosing the bad order is so that you always finish with the *good* one.

Taken to its logical conclusion this means that you lose the first game 21-0 and win the second 21-0. In the third game you are losing 10-

0, then change end and order to win 21-10. Obviously it is not so clear-cut in practice but *the order is very often the deciding factor in doubles.*

Left-handers in Doubles
A further complication is that tactics are different for a left-hander. This is because the service is always played from the right-hand side of the table (Diagram 59).

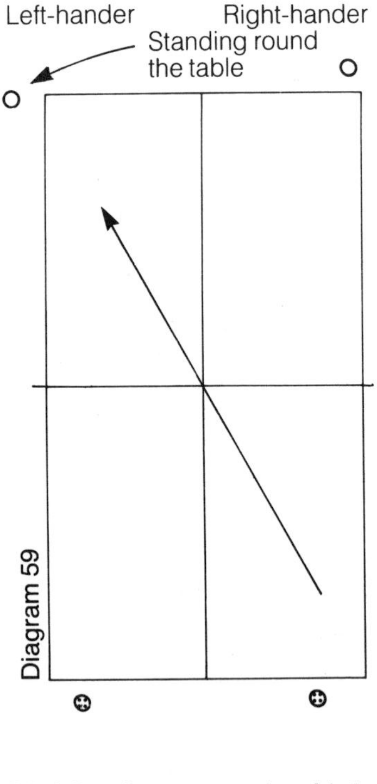

Diagram 59

A left-hander can receive this ball with his forehand by standing around the side of the table.

This makes flicking very effective and leaves the whole table free for his partner. Once into the rally the left and right-hand combination can recover to their natural positions and do not distract each other. In this way the combination can easily play forehand attacks without restriction. This makes the left and right-handed pair the most dangerous.

There could be four, three, two, one or no left-handers in any doubles match and to cover tactics for all these would take a whole book. Yet if one in six players is left-handed, the probability of having *at least* one left-hander is more than evens! This inescapable statistical fact is, for me, the straw that breaks the camel's back. The best I can advise a double pair is:

1. Serve short to avoid a fast loop return, but
2. Not too short to offer wide angles.
3. Serve with chop and float for deception but avoid sidespin as your partner will get some of your spin back.
4. Receive short services short to the forehand. This crowds the opposition at the table.
5. Attack to the X-point or preferably aim for the player who has just played to you. If you hit him with the ball the point is yours.

Personally, I like doubles and I believe there is a place in every player's training programme for serious doubles practice. I would recommend doubles as a toning-down exercise at the end of a hard session since you only play one stroke in four, instead of one in two as in singles.

Right-hander serving

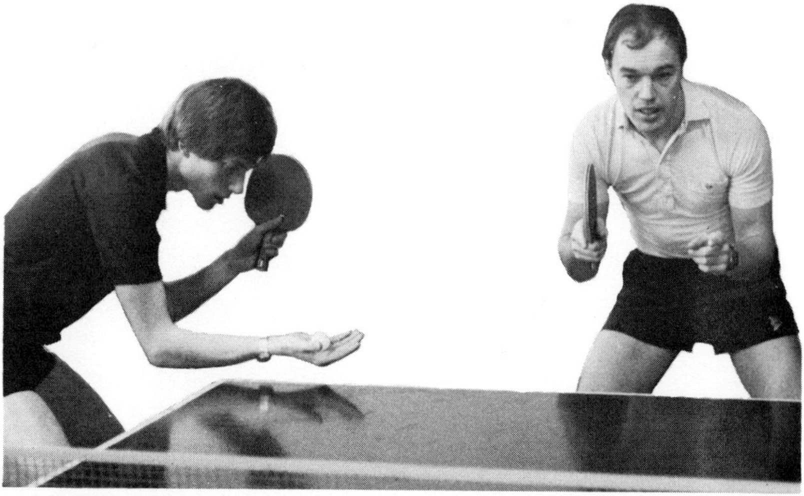

Left-hander serving

Left-hander receiving

Right-hander receiving

An Alternative Physical Programme

People may argue that table tennis is a game of speed and spin, reaction and anticipation, concentration, touch and power. It involves all these, but let's not lose our way when defining the necessary attributes. Above all else table tennis is a game of *skill*, where a player can achieve victories only within his field of skill. With the greatest knowledge, fitness and practice in the world I shall never be able to beat Des Douglas because he is in a different league of skill.

Each 'league of skill' however is fairly large and greater than most players acknowledge. For instance, in 1985 there were as many as 30 men who could fill the England No. 2 spot and on the ladies' side anyone from No. 8 upwards could win the national title.

Besides skill, a player needs preparation, mental ability, training and fitness. As previously stressed general or specific physical fitness will not make you a better table tennis player, but lack of it will make you a weaker one.

There is only one reason why a player should ever lose a match and that is because of the skill factor. No one should lose for any other reason. The most inexcusable reason is lack of effort, followed closely by lack of fitness.

Injury aside though, the out-of-condition player should be ashamed of himself for allowing this to happen and he should get to work on fitness training immediately!

This section is really intended for the player who has never experienced his top condition and so does not appreciate how limiting lack of fitness can be.

Lack of fitness may show itself in many different ways. Common problems are:

1. Fading out during the game.
2. Having to change tactics because you are out of breath and not fit enough to play the physical winning tactics.
3. An inability to play a winning game from the start due to your lack of athleticism (you may not even realize this).
4. Giving your opponent hope since he knows you are unfit. He would normally lose heart but realizes that you may tire if he 'hangs on'. In the meantime an unrelated opportunity may present itself and enable him to capitalize on a situation that would otherwise have gone unnoticed. This is common and often neither player fully realizes what has happened.
5. In order to be master of the game you should have the ability to demoralize an opponent even before the first point is played. This is achieved by *reputation* – the opponent knows he hasn't a prayer. If you are unfit he has at least one straw to clutch.

Lack of fitness may take three, five or 10 points from your game. If you are only one point below par this may turn victory into defeat in an important match, so it is a weakness well worth eliminating.

Fitness in Perspective

It is important to keep the question of fitness in a proper perspective.

Physical training should never replace relevant on-the-table training, nor should the schedule be so intricate that it becomes impractical. Some training schemes are far too elaborate for most players to adhere to them. Training programmes can be either too complex to understand or too time-consuming or based on facilities that are expensive or unavailable.

Full-time professionals training in a well-equipped gym under strict supervision can usefully work to intricate programmes. For most players, however, it is not practical to run different distances on different days, to complete circuits, shuttle-runs, sprints and go weight-training, all in addition to flexibility and table training.

Physical training should become a habit and it should include strength, speed, stamina and suppleness training which is best achieved by an all-embracing programme.

A *discontinuous* form of training is not match related. In a match your physical requirements are constantly changing, therefore you will have to develop a training programme for your particular needs. You may find it helpful to adapt the example, below, to your own needs.

Training Module

First of all decide how much time a week to put aside for physical training. Remember that you may be working within the periodisation model explained on page 22.

Balance your day-to-day work between heavy and light days. In the example on page 73, Mondays, Wednesdays and Fridays are heavy days, Tuesday and Thursday are light days. The weekends are left aside for competition or rest. You should remember that competition should not be preceded immediately by a heavy day.

Friday, as you can see, has a two hour programme so map out a long distance run of about one hour (running comfortably without a break). This will get you back to home base around one and half hours later, bearing in mind (refer to example programme) you are not just jogging.

The second part of the programme concentrates on strength training (eg pull-ups, weights etc) for 20 minutes, leaving 10 minutes for stretching and cooling down.

I have tried to ensure that the exercise circuit does not require any special apparatus. So, when you arrive back at base for progressive resistance training, you are using your own body weight or items that are around most homes, (eg chairs for dips, incline and decline press-ups, and perhaps a beam in the garage for chins and pull-ups.) In addition, you should find a basic chest expander adequate for lat pulls, bicep and leg curls.

Hungarian Tibor Klampar was the most talented European player of the seventies, and helped to pioneer the straight-arm loop technique.

Getting down on the ball with Tibor Kreisz, one of Hungary's top defensive players.

Training Module Example

Day	Monday	Tuesday	Wednesday	Thursday	Friday	Saturday/ Sunday
Total time (approx.)	1hr 45min	40min	1hr 45min	40min	2hr	
Jog	10min	8min	10min	8min	10min	
Walk	2min Shadow 3×40secs	30secs Sprint 3×10secs	2min Sprint 3×20secs	30secs Sprint 3×10secs	2min Sprint 3×20secs	
Stretch	2min	1min	2min	1min	2min	
Jog	10min	8min	10min	8min	10min	
Walk	1min Sprint 3×20secs Reverse weight sprints 4×15secs	20secs Shadow 2×30secs	1min Cat stretch 2×30secs Sit ups 2×30secs	30secs Shadow 2×30secs	1min Shadow play 3×40secs	
Stretch	2min	1min	2min	1min	2min	Flexibility only
Jog	10min	8min	10min	8min	10min	
Walk	1min Maltese cross 1min	30secs Shuttle 3×20secs	1min Shadow 3×40secs	30secs Shuttle 3×20secs	1min Shuttle 30secs Shadow 30secs Shuttle 30secs Shadow 30secs	
Stretch	2min	1min	2min	1min	2min	
Jog	10min	Mixed movement Vary pace Walk, jog, side stepping	10min	Mixed movement Vary pace Sprint, jog Walk, side stepping	10min	
Walk	1min Shadow 3×40secs		1min Shuttle 2×30secs Reverse sprints 2×30secs		1min Sit ups 40secs Trunk lifts 40secs Alternate leg raises 30 Trunk lifts 30	
Stretch	2min	5min	2min	5min	2min	
Jog	Mixed and varied pace movement Side stepping Walking Jog		Mixed and varied pace movement Sprint, jog, side stepping Walking		10min	

continued on p74

Day	Monday	Tuesday	Wednesday	Thursday	Friday	Saturday/ Sunday
Walk					1min Shadow 2×30secs Shuttle 2×30secs	
Stretch	15min		15min		2min	
Jog	Back at base		Back at base			
Walk	Heavy work Chins Pull-ups Chair dips Curls 20min		Heavy work Chins Pull-ups Chair dips Curls 20mins		Mixed movement Jogging, Sprinting, Side stepping, Walking 15mins Back at base Heavy work Pull-ups Chins Chair dips Incline and decline press ups 20mins	Flexibility only
Stretch	10min		10min		10min	

Case Studies

English Open 1984
(Men's Singles Final)
Desmond Douglas (England) v Vladislav Broda (Czechoslovakia).
Even though Des had very modest results in the team event he started clear favourite in looking for his third Open title.

Broda, a twin, was really the dark horse in the final, having come through from an unseeded position. The question was whether Broda's left-handed attacking play and awkward service would trouble Des.

No UK player had beaten Des in nearly eight years and on only three occasions did he have problems. The players extending Des were Paul Day, Kevin Beadsley and Graham Sandley.

The common denominator was that all these are left-handers like Broda and the matches against Day and Sandley were over five games. Generally speaking Des is not so good against left-handers and not so good over five games.

The Match
In a short-rallied game Broda quickly took the initiative, troubling Des with his high toss serve which was beating Des in both width and length. Firstly, it was pitching

between backhand and forehand causing indecision and secondly the length was near perfect for a half-long service.

As a result Des played some very unsettled table tennis against the serve. He failed to return many serves at all and played such weak returns on others that Broda was able to win points with his powerful loop-drive immediately behind his service (see the analysis chart on page 27).

After Broda won the first two games convincingly a change of tactics was inevitable. Des, deciding on a more positive approach to the service, committed himself to receive service with his forehand, usually before the ball had even pitched. It soon became obvious that when Des returned the service effectively, he held the advantage in the longer rallies (see Diagram 60).

The tactic worked. With more consistent play both with and against the service, Des took the next two games 21-12, 21-7.

In the fifth game, the players changed ends at 10-7 to Broda but Des's early commitment on the return, together with a foul service from Broda, threw the Czech off his stride. Douglas took a lead of 17-13 and then won four of the next five points with service to emerge the victor 21-14.

Why does Des struggle against fellow left-handers?

Douglas is by nature a world-class blocker (both on attack and in defence). Like most blockers he is stronger on the backhand.

The right-hander naturally plays his (stronger) forehand into Des's backhand which is advantageous to him as a blocker. The left-hander naturally attacks diagonally to Des's forehand block which is more dangerous for Desmond.

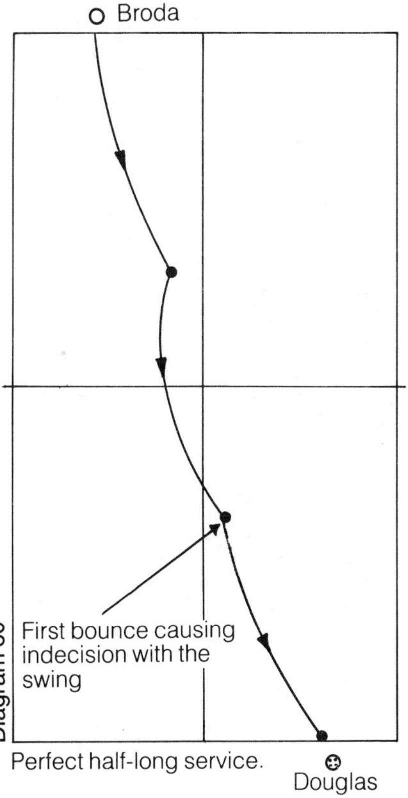

Diagram 60
Perfect half-long service.

Why does Des struggle over five games?

I feel Des is so quick that an opponent is likely to lose against him before even warming-up to his speed. In a five game match, however, there is more time to adjust to his lightning speed of play. This makes his recovery against Broda rather exceptional – Des demonstrated the importance of good tactical thinking.

1984 European Youth Championships
Boys' Singles Final
Andrei Mazunov (USSR) v Carl Prean (England)
The 1984 final predictably brought together two highly talented and unorthodox favourites. Mazunov had recently reached the semi-finals of the 1984 European Men's Championships while Prean had more than helped England to fourth place in the 1983 World Championships.

The rule change forced Prean to play with two different coloured rubbers which was obviously a handicap to the combination bat player.

The question being asked was whether Prean could contain or prevent Mazunov's brilliant backhand loop by keeping the ball short or playing wide to the angles. Mazunov would undoubtedly try to play this stroke if he were able to combat the combination skills of Prean but would he cope with Prean's forehand, which offers virtually no cues or clues for anticipation (Diagram 61).

This is how England Captain Donald Parker viewed the match:

The first problem was to put Carl in the right frame of mind. Often in a final a player is too nervous and therefore *just* keeps the ball on the table. If Carl adopted these tactics, relying on Mazunov's mistakes, he stood no chance of winning.

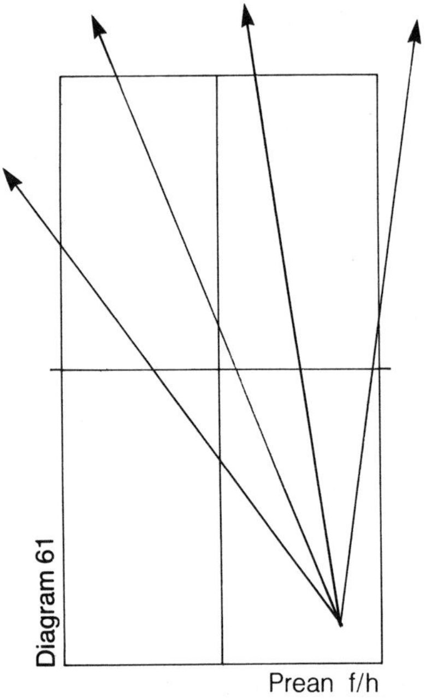

Diagram 61

Carl Prean capable of playing his f/h anywhere without detection.

It was vital that Carl stayed close to the table. If Mazunov forced Carl back the Russian would win the loop-to-loop rallies, so Carl needed to 'stay up' and drive or topspin *early*. On the backhand Carl would need to 'twiddle' his bat to give different spins and also play down the lines more than usual.

Close to the table Mazunov has a strong backhand flick and loop and uses these sometimes even from his forehand side. He tends to *overstep* though, leaving his backhand exposed.

Carl exploited Mazunov's overstepping by serving short and wide to the forehand. If Mazunov used his backhand then Carl would then attack hard to his opponent's open backhand wing (Diagram 62).

A fast service to the Russian's backhand would also tend to unbalance Mazunov, giving him too much ground to cover with his backhand. As a result Carl won the first game and took a lead in the second.

Mazunov however has a great fighting spirit and chose to serve long. This avoided the possibility of Carl returning service short and enabled Mazunov to follow up with strong topspin loops to win the second game. In the third and final game Prean again went ahead but could not attack Mazunov's service as hard as he wanted. Mazunov's spirit and Prean's slightly negative play was enough for the Russian to recover and win the match 21-19.

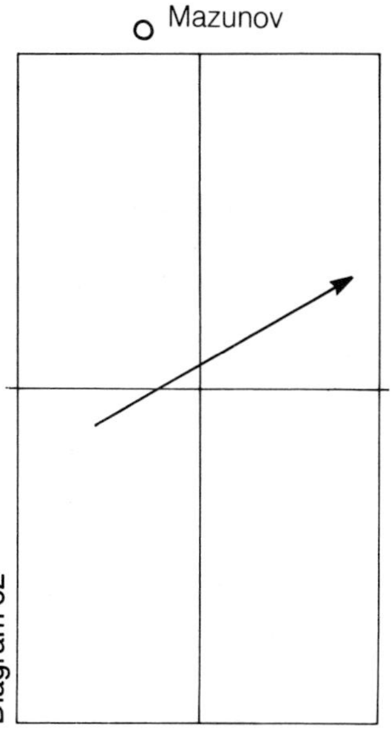

Diagram 62

Mazunov's stance favours his b/h play, but leaves the wide b/h court exposed.

1983 World Championships (Tokyo)
Men's Singles Final
Guo Yue Hua (China) v Cai Zhen Hui (China)

No technical or tactical book would be complete without a study of three times world finalist and current World Champion Guo Yue Hua, the most complete and composed player, simply the greatest of them all.

The younger Cai Zhen Hui who is the current World No. 1 was favoured by many. Could his speed and aggression tire the reigning World Champion?

It was interesting to note the clash of styles. Guo is a right-handed pen-grip player and Cai is a left-handed Western-grip player.

This was not such a spectacle as some earlier matches as most rallies were finished by the sixth ball. It was nevertheless a final for the perfectionist – technically and tactically nearly perfect.

Diagram 63

Both players served mainly with the forehand from the backhand court (see Diagram 63).

After losing the first game 21-15, Cai played with more aggression, pressurizing Guo with his bulldozer approach. He attacked earlier and looked to finish the rallies quickly. By switching Guo wide on both wings he forced Guo to play his weaker backhand. This is a general tactic against the penholder. Cai took the second game 21-19 (see Diagram 64).

In the third game Guo, with immaculate footwork, covered 80% of the table with his forehand. His tactics were text-book material. When serving he always followed with an aggressive forehand, usually from the backhand side, across the diagonal. This forced Cai Zhen to reach wide to his forehand. If Cai returned this Guo would attack the opposite court and this usually concluded the rally.

When receiving service Guo played many outright winners, down the line, passing Cai's forehand. Guo is possibly the only player in the world who can do this and he did so with such precision. Watching the game it was amazing how Cai managed to accumulate 18 points (Diagram 65).

Guo began the fourth game with very similar tactics – possibly with a small modification. If Cai had the audacity to stay in the rally Guo would conclude with a winning ball into the X-point. This was interesting as it is usually a second to fifth-ball tactic yet Guo only used it to terminate a relatively long rally (see Diagram 66).

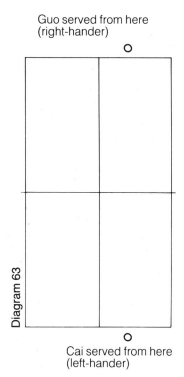

Cai tried desperately to alter the course of the match. He attacked Guo's service long into the backhand, and in the rallies he knew switching was his best tactic.

Yet Guo's brilliance shone through and his fitness and technique never wavered. He even had time to topspin-lob from (10m) behind the table!

Guo took the fourth game 21-18 to retain the World Championship. Sadly it was to be his last as he retired from competitive play after the event.

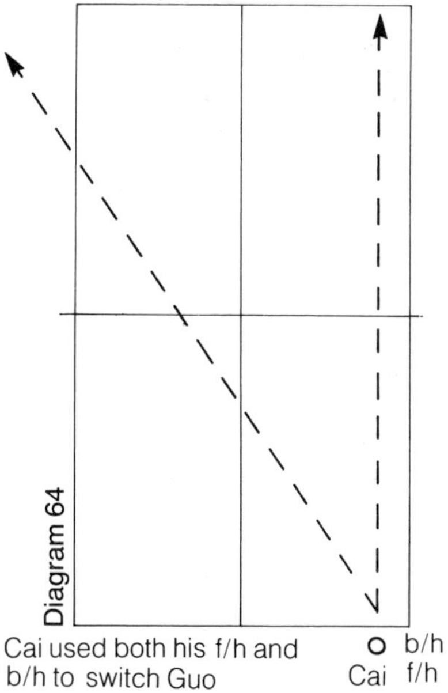

Diagram 64

Cai used both his f/h and b/h to switch Guo

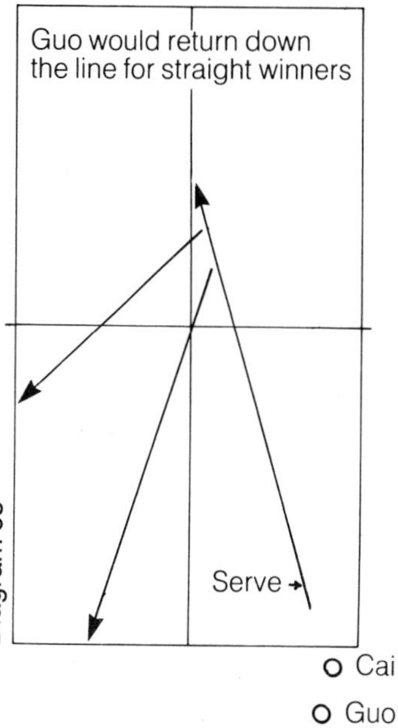

Diagram 65

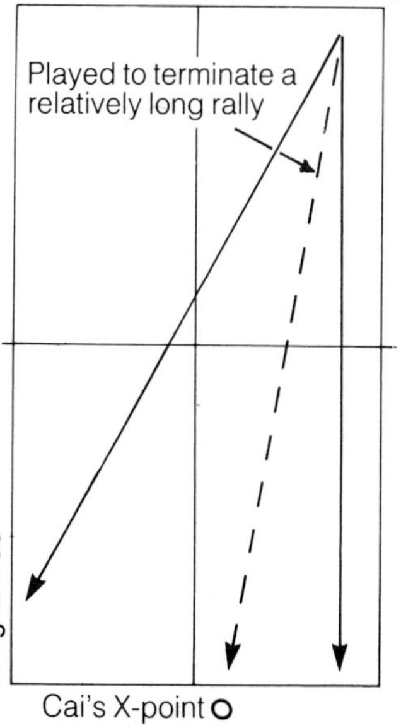

Diagram 66

Conclusion: 21 up

Throughout this book I have emphasized the importance of acquiring a solid foundation to your play by learning the technique first and by applying tactics later.

No one book could ever claim to contain every tactic available to the table tennis player, but I have tried to cover the main, basic tactics and the more subtle tactics of the game.

It is now up to you as a player to adopt and apply what you have learned in this book and thereby enhance your own particular style. But remember that there is no 'total tactic' – there will always be a player who can combat any one tactic you may apply. Equally, there will never be a player who can combat all tactics.

Try to remember your tactical boxes and to slip in and out of them undetected.

The total tactician has a bank of tactics. He selects the winning tactics, cunningly moves in and out of his tactical boxes undetected, improvises effectively, is very decisive in his choice of tactics and recognizes instantly and instinctively which tactical boxes do not apply to any specific game. He is the 'Master of the Game'. I hope you can be master of your game. Good luck!

Table Measurements

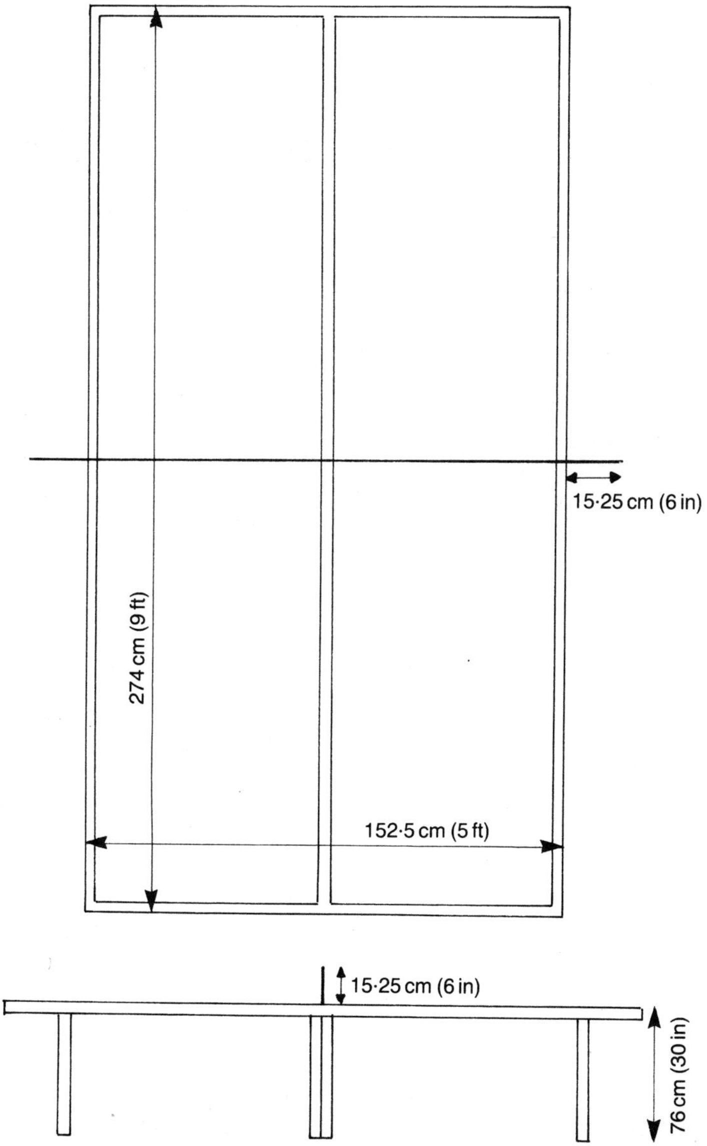

Tibor Klampar (Hungary) displays tactical alertness by moving around his b/h court. The diagonal f/h loop leaves Li Chen Shi (China) standing.

Dunlop Skills Award Scheme

Rules for Grade One

Note: Throughout the test the following abbreviations will be used to denote specific areas on the table. (see diagram)
B=Backhand Contact area
F=Forehand Contact area
BT=Backhand Target area
FT=Forehand Target area
A sheet of A3 paper (or 2 pieces of A4) are ideal for indicating size of target area and can be moved to suit the test.

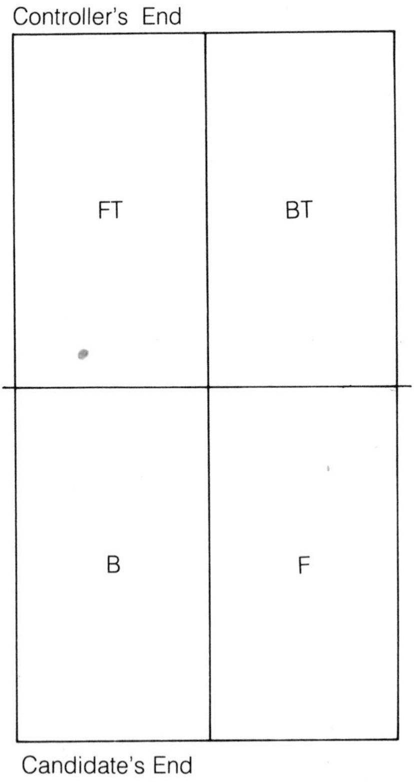

Test 1: Objective—to improve "feel" of bat and ball
(No table is needed for this test.)
Demonstrates forehand tap bounce.
Pass: 10 bounces with maximum one error. (3 attempts allowed)

Test 2: Objective—to improve "feel" of bat and ball
As test 1, played with backhand.

Test 3: Objective—to improve stance and alertness
(Any table can be used for this test.)
Demonstrate a good "ready" position; slightly crouched, knees slightly bent. Feet apart, more than shoulder width. Bat held lightly, pointing at and ready to track an imaginary on-coming ball.

Test 4: Objective—to improve skill in guiding (not "hitting") the ball
Candidate drops ball from 10" (25cm) height at position B and steers it backhand to BT. Controller catches and returns the ball.
Pass: 10 balls with maximum 2 errors. (3 attempts allowed)

Test 5: Objective—to improve skill in guiding (not "hitting") the ball
Exactly as Test 4 but dropping the ball at position F and steering it forehand to FT.

Test 6: Objective—to improve mobility
(Again, any table of suitable width can be used for this test.) Demonstrate 6 movements to either side, F to B, with bat but without ball.
Pass: Use of small skip-steps, moving on toes and never closing feet.

Test 7: Objective—to improve understanding of position
Demonstrate ability to steer balls alternately, backhand B to BT and forehand F to FT.
Procedure: Candidate drops ball to bounce net-high at B and steers smoothly backhand to BT. Candidate then moves to F and catches ball thrown there by Controller. Candidate then drops ball at F and steers it forehand to FT. Moves back to B to catch ball thrown by Controller. And so on. Test continues until 20 alternate steering actions have been played.
Pass: 20 alternate steering actions with no more than 5 errors.

Test 8: Objective—to encourage the idea of partnership in learning
Pass: Candidate must act as Controller (eg catcher and thrower) to another Grade One Candidate. Assessor to judge co-operation and team spirit etc.

This completes Grade One.

General Notes
For "Penholder" styles read "to the left of the body" for "backhand".
When assessing left-handed candidates, reverse all targets.

Rules for Grade Two

Test 1: Objective—to practice "receive" of mini-service
Note: Always make it clear that the "Mini-Serve" is a slow, short practice ball to improve touch and placing, and is NOT A CORRECT MATCH SERVICE (contact only with opponent's side of table).
Procedure: Backhand return from B to BT against Controller's Mini-Serve BT to B.
Pass: 4 out of 5 balls, correctly returned to Controller, and not beyond area BT. (3 attempts allowed)

Test 2: Objective—as Test 1
Procedure: Forehand returns (F to FT) of Controller's Mini-Serves (FT to F).
Pass: As Test 1.

Test 3: Objective—the practice of "good returns"
Procedure: Play 10 successive continuous slow-speed returns with Forehand from half-court F to half-court FT, and half-court BT, alternately. Controller or approved Partner must return slow speed, all balls to F.
Pass: Maximum 1 error. (3 attempts allowed) An error by a Controller does not count against the Candidate, who can continue his score.

Test 4: Objective—as Test 3
Procedure: Play with Backhand from half-court B to half-court BT, and FT, alternately.
Pass: As Test 3.

Test 5: Objective—similar to Test 3
Procedure: Candidate must make 16 slow-speed returns, alternating Forehand with Backhand.
Pass: Maximum 2 errors. (Controller should not put Candidate under pressure)

Test 6: Objective—to assess candidate's T.T. knowledge
Answer questions about: (i) A correct Table (ii) A correct Net (iii) A correct Bat (iv) Procedures in case of a Net-ball (v) Regulations about Clothing.

This completes Grade Two.

General Notes
For "Penholder" styles read "to the left of the body" for "backhand".
When assessing left-handed candidates, reverse all targets.

As the Grade Two Award deals with developing rally skills a steady Controller is needed; this may be the Assessor, or a more experienced junior under supervision.

Rules for Grade Three

Note: Throughout the test the following abbreviations will be used to denote specific areas on the table. (see diagram)
B=Backhand Contact area
F=Forehand Contact area
BT=Backhand Target area
FT=Forehand Target area
A sheet of A3 paper (or 2 pieces of A4) are ideal for indicating size of target area and can be moved to suit the test.

Test 1: All-backhand push control (From 2 points, returning to 1 Target)
Using sound footwork for training, return 30 Slow Push Shots (which have been placed, slowly, by Controller from C1, alternately, to Area B and Area M). Candidate to use only BACKHAND PUSH-STROKES, all played back to Area C1.
Pass: 30 successes before 4th error.

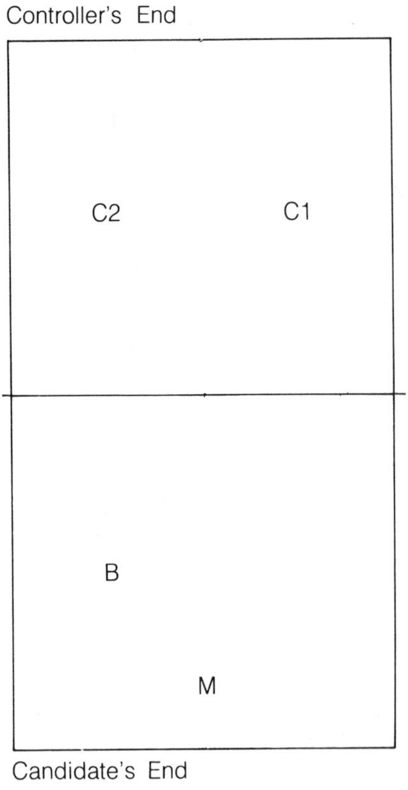

Test 2: All forehand controlled top-spin drive
Against steady returns from Controller, play 30 FOREHAND DRIVE strokes, maintaining direction on 1 diagonal only, without increasing speed.
Pass: 30 successes before 4th error.

Test 3: Combined control
Return 30 slow balls from Controller by playing, in strict alternation BACKHAND PUSH and FOREHAND DRIVE.
Note: Controller should feed balls alternately to B and M
Pass: 30 successes before 4th error.

Test 4: Backhand "block" returns
Against medium speed Topspin from Controller, return ball by simple rebound technique, ie straight-line "reflection", from the peak-of-bounce position. Maintain direction on 1 diagonal.
Pass: 30 successes before 4th error.

Test 5: Short-touch services
(i) From correct position behind the baseline serve Short FOREHAND Services so as to clear the net and bounce twice on the table.
(ii) As (i) but service with BACKHAND.
Pass: In each case, 5 successes to be achieved within 8 attempts.

Test 6: Long topspin services
(i) From correct position, serve with FOREHAND, ball to land beyond Target Area C2.
(ii) As (i) service with BACKHAND, ball to land beyond Target Area C1.
Pass: In each case, 5 successes within 8 attempts.

This completes Grade Three.

General Notes
For "Penholder" styles read "to the left of the body" for "backhand".
When assessing left-handed candidates, reverse all targets.

Rules for Matchplayer Level

Notes: (i) This level can only be assessed by ETTA Club or Diploma Coaches.
(ii) Candidates must already have passed the Grade Three Award.
(iii) The Assessor must satisfy him/herself that the quality of the candidates stroke work is satisfactory.
(iv) Before scoring each test the Assessor must witness and approve a "dry land" demonstration of the ensuing stroke action(s).

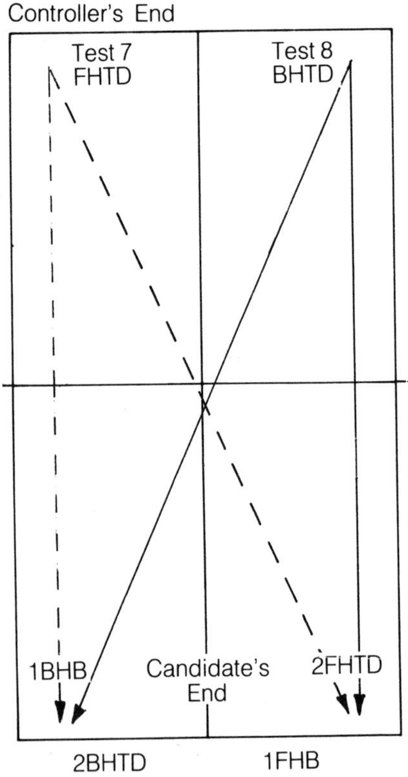

(v) Throughout the test the following abbreviations will be used.
FHTD=Forehand Top Spin Drive
BHTD=Backhand Top Spin Drive
FHB=Forehand Block
BHB=Backhand Block

Test 1: Return of varied services
Required: Suitable push or attack Services delivered with medium strength Sidespins, including elements of Topspin and Chop.
Pass: 16 successes before 5th error.

Test 2: Services variation
Deliver Services of varying strength, incorporating Sidespin, alternating Left and Right.
Pass: 16 successes before 5th error.

Test 3: Combining drive-and-push—forehand
Return 30 balls, which have been alternately pushed and chopped, by using (respectively) Topspin Drive and Short Push-Shots, played alternately, Forehand, on one diagonal line. Topspin and Backspin must be clearly displayed in the rallies.
Pass: 30 correct before 5th error.

Test 4: Combining drive-and-push—backhand
As Test 3 but using Backhand throughout.
Pass: As Test 3.

Test 5: Combining (chopped) defensive returns with push—forehand
Return 30 balls which have been alternately driven and pushed, on same line, by using, respectively Backspin Defensive Returns and

Short Pushes, played alternately on same line, all FOREHAND. Topspin and Backspin must be clearly displayed in the Rallies.
Pass: As Test 3.

Test 6: Combining (chopped) defensive returns with push—backhand
As Test 5 but using BACKHAND throughout.
Pass: As Test 3.

Test 7: Maintaining attack against topspin from Controller
Maintain 10 triple sequences thus:
2 FOREHAND TOPSPIN Drives plus
1 BACKHAND Block.
Pass: 10 good sequences before 5th error.

Test 8: As Test 7 but
Sequences of 2 BACKHAND drives plus 1 forehand block.
Pass: 10 good sequences before 5th error.

Test 9: Laws and Rules
Answer 10 "everyday" questions on Laws and match procedure. Points allowed: For complete answer 3; for correct "sense" 2; for a part answer 1.
Pass: Score 22 out of 30.

This completes the Matchplayer Award.

General Notes
For "Penholder" styles read "to the left of the body" for "backhand".
When assessing left-handed candidates, reverse all targets.

Rules for Masters Level

Notes: (i) This level can only be assessed by ETTA Diploma Coaches.
(ii) Candidates must already have passed the Matchplayer Award.
(iii) The Candidate must have the approval of an ETTA. Diploma Coach as to general level of playing ability and presentation.
(iv) The Candidate must pass NINE tests of his/her own selection from the twelve available.

Controller's End

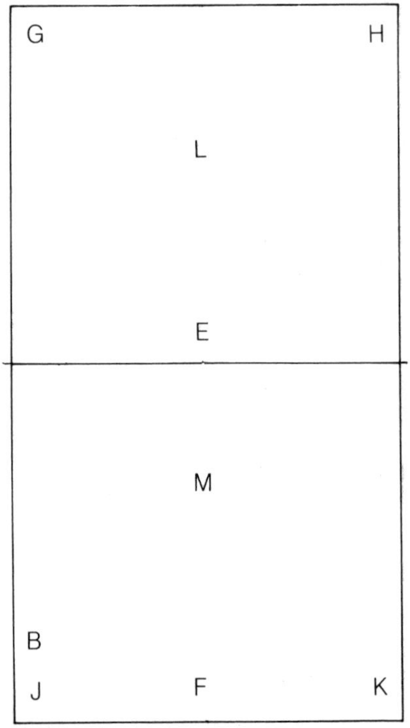

Candidate's End

Test 1: Topspin driving under pressure, forehand and backhand
Play 30 alternate Topspin Drives, to one point, against Half-volley returns which have been placed alternately to Areas F and B. Good position and footwork required throughout.
Pass: 30 correct before 3rd error.

Test 2: Counter-driving, close and distant, forehand
Return 30 Counter-Drives by means of Forehand Counter-Drives in sequences of 2 thus: 2 "Close", 2 "Distant", 2 "Close", etc. All returns kept on the same diagonal.
Pass: 3rd error fails.

Test 3: Counter-driving, close and distant, backhand
As Test 2 but using Backhand Counter-Drive.
Pass: 3rd error fails.

Test 4: Combining forehand & backhand topspin drives
Against slow chopped returns, which have been placed alternately to Areas J and K, by playing 20 Forehand and Backhand Topspin Drives, alternately directed diagonally to Areas H and G.
Pass: 3rd error fails.

Test 5: Combining forehand & backhand defensive backspin returns
Return 20 Drives, received alternately on Corner Areas J and K by means of, respectively, Forehand and Backhand Chopped returns, to Area L.
Pass: 3rd error fails.

Test 6: Sequences of topspin-and-backspin strokes
Play 15 double sequences of Forehand Chop and Backhand Drive against balls which have been respectively Driven to the Forehand and Pushed to the Backhand and returned to Area G.
Pass: 4th error fails.

Test 7: Sequences of topspin-and-backspin strokes
Play the reverse of Test 6 ie "Backhand" for "Forehand" and vice versa. Return to Area H.
Pass: 4th error fails.

Test 8: Backhand attack "distribution"
Play 10 triple sequences thus: Drop-shot to Area E. Backhand Drive to Area H. Backhand Drive to Area G; and repeat etc. Controller returns all balls to Area M with Backspin. Candidate may keep ball in play with simple placing shots between the actual "scoring" sequences.
Pass: 4th error fails.

Test 9: Display understanding of loop-topspin, forehand
Play 8 double sequences thus: "9 o'clock loop" against chopped return followed by "12 o'clock loop" against Blocked return.
Sequence must be according to opportunity, a continuous Rally is not demanded.
Pass: 3rd error fails.

Test 10: Triple sequences
Play 10 triple sequences of Backhand Topspin Drive, Forehand Loop and Forehand Drive to area L, from balls which have been Blocked by the Controller to areas J, F and K respectively.
Pass: 4th error fails.

Test 11: 3rd ball attack
Deliver 10 Backhand services of varying lengths and spin which are to be flicked or pushed alternately to K and J. The candidate must follow up with a suitable 3rd ball attack.
Pass: 4th error fails.

Test 12: as Test 11 but Forehand serves.
Pass: 4th error fails.

Useful Addresses

International Bodies

European Table Tennis Union
43 Knowsley Road
Smithills
Bolton
Lancashire BL1 6JH
Tel: 0204 42223

International Table Tennis Federation
53 London Road
St Leonards-on-Sea
East Sussex TN37 6AY
Tel: 0424 43 0971

UK National Bodies

English Table Tennis Association
21 Claremont
Hastings
East Sussex TN34 1HA
Tel: 0424 43 3121

Irish Table Tennis Association
4 Fairhill Gardens
Belfast BT15 4FZ
Tel: 0232 77608

Scottish Table Tennis Association
18 Ainslie Place
Edinburgh EH3 6AU
Tel: 031 225 3020

Table Tennis Association of Wales
198 Cynoed Road
Cardiff CF2 6BQ
Tel: 0222 757241

English Schools' Table Tennis Association
Engelberg
Badger Lane
Woolly Moor
Derbyshire

Index